Contents

INTRODUCTION AND ACKNOWLEDGEMENTS

D1340238

This guide is intended for the owners of all sorts of flats, whether you have bought a tenement flat, a modern flat, a conversion or your own council flat. The same basic rules apply to everyone but different problems may arise in different types of flats in different parts of the country and these will be dealt with as we go along.

Introduction

Most of us have probably at some time had problems with neighbours. We all know that a good relationship with neighbours can make life easier and more pleasant and that a difficult relationship can make life a misery. Getting on with neighbours is especially important when living in a flat and sharing facilities, whether a common hall, or garden, or stairway.

If part of a shared building needs repair, who is responsible? Whose job is it to instruct tradesmen? Who pays? Do those living on the ground floor have to pay for new downpipes? Do those living on the top floor have to share the gardening? Who pays for improvements to the paintwork in the common stairway? Whose roof is it anyway?

These are just some of the questions which regularly arise for flat owners. They reflect a peculiarly Scottish style of home ownership introduced centuries ago with tenements or "stanelands". But whether you live in a flat in such a tenement block or a new flat, a large house converted into flats or a flat bought from the Council, you will be faced with very similar problems. This booklet is an attempt to help.

The Scottish Consumer Council first started to consider the problems of flat-owners by looking at the way in which the factoring system worked in Glasgow and the west of Scotland. For historical reasons, many flats in Glasgow are "factored"; that is, the owners jointly employ an agent, the factor, to arrange repairs and maintenance for them.

The factoring system is, in theory, a very sensible way of dealing with the problems of common repairs. However, when we asked for owners' views on the system we discovered a high level of dissatisfaction. One of the main reasons for this dissatisfaction is that owners do not know where they stand or what they can expect from their factor. And this, in turn, causes difficulties for the factors.

We next looked at how flat owners in other parts of Scotland dealt with repairs and maintenance. Again we discovered problems and dissatisfaction, and again this is largely because owners do not know where they stand.

It is clear to us that the major problem faced by all flat-owners is that they do not have enough information about their rights and responsibilities. They do not know their position when it comes to getting repairs done, what their relationship is with their factor if they have one, what their rights are in relation to their neighbours, and so on. The main aim of this booklet is therefore to inform flat owners about their rights and responsibilities. It also explains what flat-owners can do to ensure that repairs are done to their satisfaction and that their building is properly maintained. It gives advice on sources of help: practical help from surveyors and factors; financial help in the form of local authority grants and loans; how to get help and advice from solicitors or advice agencies.

At the end of the day, however, the crucial lesson is that it is up to the owners themselves to look after their buildings. Owners must be prepared to spend time and thought and, of course, money to ensure that their property is kept in good condition. Owners must be prepared to help themselves and we hope this booklet will encourage them.

Esme Walker,
Chairman, Scottish Consumer Council.

Acknowledgements

This booklet was commissioned and funded by the Scottish Consumer Council. It was researched and written by Sheila Gilmore and edited by Eveline Hunter, to whom our thanks. It was prepared for publication by Margaret Burns and Finella Wilson. We are also grateful to the Property Owners and Factors Association of Glasgow, Janey Tucker, Ann Flint and all those who commented on drafts.

1
Owning a flat

Owning a flat is a lot more complicated than owning a house. When you buy a house you only have to look after your own property, but when you buy a flat you are also taking on a share with the other owners of maintaining all the common parts of the building. These can include the roof, the shared entrance, the stairs, the outside walls and, in some cases, cleaning and caretaking services.

Every flat owner has some legal responsibility towards the repair and maintenance of these shared areas and services. That means you also have to pay your share of the upkeep costs.

In many cases the arrangement works out reasonably well, with each owner chipping in regularly to keep the place going. But as many flat owners will confirm, not all owners are as interested in the property as they should be. And when problems arise they can be a real headache.

The owners may have to agree amongst themselves what repairs are necessary and what tradesmen to use, but getting agreement from sometimes as many as twelve different households is by no means easy. Sometimes the owners cannot agree on what repairs are necessary or some want to do more improvement work than others. Some owners may not care about the state of the property at all and would quite happily let it deteriorate rather than spend any of their own money. Owners like that can hold up essential repairs for ages and infuriate the others who want to get the work done as soon as possible. Even when agreement has been reached it can be difficult getting money from some owners and this can involve the others, or the factor if there is one, in a lot of extra effort and expense.

Many flatted properties, especially in Glasgow and the West of Scotland, have factors to look after repairs and maintenance. This is very common in old tenement buildings in Glasgow but is also popular in modern blocks of flats throughout Scotland.

In theory having a factor should make life easier for the owners but in practice there are a lot of complaints about the way factors operate, particularly in old tenement buildings. Some flat owners complain that the factor charges too much money for his services, that there are unnecessary delays in getting work done, or that if the work is faulty they have little comeback on the factor. Factors on the other hand have complained that some owner-occupiers are totally uninterested in the state of their property, and that some refuse to pay their share of the costs or take so long in paying that the factor has to incur extra expense.

These are the kinds of problems this booklet tries to deal with. But before going on to specific problems it is important to understand exactly what your rights and obligations are as a flat owner. The following section describes the legal position and you may need to refer to it again later when you read the other chapters.

Your legal duties as a flat owner

It would be nice if we could say that there are clearcut rules governing who is responsible for doing what in a flatted property, but unfortunately there are not. There are rules in the ordinary common law of Scotland but in most cases these do not apply because each flat has its own title deeds.

Title deeds explain, among other things, what common areas of the building you have the right to use and for which you are responsible, what share of the maintenance you have to pay, how decisions should be reached among the various owners, and whether or not you have to employ a factor to look after the property.

These important legal documents determine your rights and duties towards the building. Your flat will have title deeds whether it is in a tenement, a modern block, a converted house or a council housing estate. All title deeds are different, though there are certain similarities between them.

Occasionally the title deeds make no reference to the repair and maintenance of the property. In these cases the ordinary common law of Scotland applies but since they are unusual they are dealt with at the end of the chapter.

What is so important about title deeds?

Title deeds are the documents which were drawn up when the building was first sold and they lay down conditions for all future owners. They cover such things as rights to the land the property was built on and rights to various parts of the building itself.

The word "rights" is rather misleading because for every right you have a duty. If you have a right to use the common entrance and stairs to get to your flat you have a corresponding duty to help keep them in good repair.

Besides setting out the responsibilities for repairs and maintenance the deeds usually lay down other restrictions, such as prohibitions against the use of flats for commercial purposes and limitations on the kind of extensions or alterations that can be made to the building. Since most of these things are now covered by planning laws they are of less importance to the average owner-occupier than the rules relating to maintenance and the sharing of bills.

Who decides what needs to be done?

Most deeds say that agreement from all the owners, or at least a majority of them, is needed before any decisions can be reached. This would include decisions about repairs and improvements, employing or dismissing a factor, arranging common insurance or anything else that affects the common interests of owners.

In Edinburgh most deeds say that ALL owners have to agree before any action is taken. In Glasgow it is more common for the agreement of a majority of owners to be enough. Usually a simple majority is sufficient but sometimes the deeds say that a certain proportion of the owners must consent before the decision is binding.

If you have a factor the deeds will usually give him power to take decisions on your behalf without consulting ANY of the owners.

Since the title deeds are so important in deciding how decisions are reached you should as an owner try to see them for yourself. Later in this chapter we explain how to get a copy of your deeds and how to get help in understanding them.

What Share of the Costs Do I Pay?

All title deeds describe the areas of the building that are common. You should have free and unrestricted access to them, though that also means you should not restrict the access of other owners to these common areas. The deeds also specify what your share of the costs are.

There are three main ways of allocating each owner's share of the costs.

* Each owner pays an equal share. So if there are eight owners you will pay one-eighth of the cost of repairs, improvements and maintenance, etc.

* Each owner pays according to the rateable value of his flat. So, if your rateable value is £200 and the total rateable value of all the flats amounts to £2,000, you will pay 200/2,000, which is of course a tenth of all the bills.

* Sometimes the feu duty is used instead of the rateable value, although this is less common. Your proportion of the feu duty would be your proportion of the bills. Most flat owners have now bought out their feu obligations but this makes no difference to how your share of the bills is worked out.

But some title deeds allocate costs in other ways.

The most common arrangement in the deeds is for all owners to share the costs equally. Only by looking at the deeds for your flat, however, can you be sure what arrangement applies to you.

Title deeds and factors

Some deeds, especially in Glasgow and the West of Scotland, state that a factor may be appointed and lay down rules for how that factor should be appointed and what his powers and duties will be. Even if there is no such provision, it is still open to a group of flat owners to appoint a factor.

Occasionally the deeds stipulate that a factor MUST be appointed and even name the factor. But, provided that ALL owners agree, this does not stop you changing your factor or doing without a factor at all. If, however, one or more of the owners don't agree to a change you will have to continue to employ the factor named in your title deeds.

The deeds will say what the factor's responsibilities are. Usually he can take decisions on the owners' behalf WITHOUT CONSULTING THEM BEFOREHAND. This is because legally he is your agent and you have given him permission to act on your behalf, to instruct tradesmen and to pay the bills. You are legally bound by any agreements he has entered into on your behalf and you cannot get out of paying bills just because you were not consulted beforehand. If however he has done something which the owners have specifically told him not to do they may be able to claim money back from the factor.

Many flat owners have reached written agreements with their factors about how things should be done and when the owners should be consulted. These agreements are legally binding on both factor and owner. They are discussed in chapter 8. If you buy a flat and the previous owner had a written agreement with a factor which covered things not dealt with in the title deeds it is up to you to decide whether or not you want to continue with the details of this agreement. But you do have to abide by any conditions in your title deeds.

If you do live in a factored flat or are thinking about factoring you should read chapters 5, 6, 7 and 8.

How do I get a copy of my title deeds?

It is not very difficult to get a copy of or to have a look at your deeds. You can get them from your solicitor, your building society or Register House in Edinburgh. (see address below).

The best time to find out about the rules which apply to your flat is when you buy it. Some solicitors give you what is called a ''Note On Title'' which briefly lists the rules in the deeds. You should ask your solicitor to give you a ''Note on Title''. But you can ask for a full copy of the deeds if you want to. You don't need copies of all the deeds just those which set out the conditions relating to the property.

After you have bought the flat the deeds are usually kept by the building society or bank which gave you the mortgage. Generally they will give you a copy if asked to; though they may make a charge for this. If you have no mortgage the deeds will probably have been kept by your solicitor.

As a last resort, all title deeds are recorded in the Register of Scotland and copies are kept at Register House, Meadowbank House, 143 London Road, Edinburgh EH8 7AU. You have to pay a fee for looking at the deeds and also for photocopying them.

You can choose either to write to Register House, giving your name, address and the description of the flat (for example, "one up left"), or to go there in person between the hours of 10am and 4pm. You will probably need to have information looked up for you. A "search fee" will be charged but this is seldom more than £10 depending on how far back you need to go. If you write to Register House they will send you an estimate of the cost.

I've got the deeds but I don't understand them

Don't worry! Most people can make neither head nor tail of their title deeds without spending a great deal of time over them. They tend to be written in obscure legal language but, if you are serious about standing up for your rights as a flat owner, you should make the effort to get them and find out what they mean. It's not as hard as it might seem at first.

The most obvious source of advice is your own solicitor, though he will probably charge you for his services. If the solicitor you use is the one who did your conveyancing he is unlikely to charge an extra fee for explaining what the deeds mean, though he is entitled to do so.

Other sources of help in interpreting the document include Citizens' Advice Bureaux and other advice centres. In any case, don't be disheartened. You don't have to understand all the gobbledegook about Lord Such and Such who owned the land in 1803 (title deeds are full of things like that) as long as you can work out how many owners are needed before decisions can be made, what your share of the costs is and whether or not you have to use a factor. Read it several times and common sense will see you through the important bits.

What if there is nothing in the deeds?

In cases where the deeds say nothing about responsibilities for repairs and maintenance, the ordinary common law of Scotland applies. Here is a summary of some of its rules:

* The roof is mainly the responsibility of the top floor flat owners and they are obliged to keep the part of the roof above their flats in good repair for the protection of everyone else.

Any parts of the roof above the common stair is the responsibility of all the owners. So the top floor flat owners have to pay for most of the roof repairs.

* The front garden and back garden and everything below the ground are owned by the ground floor flat owners and they have to pay for all the repairs needed there.

* The passage and stairs belong to every owner who has the right to pass through them. Each of them therefore has to share in the cost of maintaining them.

* Each owner is responsible only for the part of the outside wall which encloses his flat and for the internal walls of his flat.

* The floor and ceiling of each flat are divided by an imaginary line drawn through the middle of the joists, so that you are responsible only for your own ceilings and floors and half the floor joists between your neighbour and yourself.

REMEMBER THAT THESE RULES APPLY ONLY TO PEOPLE WHO HAVE NOTHING IN THEIR TITLE DEEDS ABOUT REPAIRS AND MAINTENANCE.

I've bought a modern flat — do the same rules apply?

When people think of a flat they still often think of the older tenement properties typical of the Scottish cities, but nowadays flat owners are almost as likely to be living in a custom-built modern block as in a tenement.

Whether your property is old or modern the same rules apply. Your modern flat will have title deeds which set out your rights and obligations towards the common parts of the building, how decisions are reached between the owners and whether or not you have to appoint a factor or agent.

The deeds vary from property to property and it is just as important for a modern flat owner to see a copy as it is for other flat owners. You should ask to see the conditions when you first buy the flat.

What will the deeds say?

Sometimes there are two sets of conditions: general ones governing the sale of the property and specifying your rights towards the common areas, and more detailed conditions about the running of the property. The Scottish Consumer Council got copies from several Scottish builders of the conditions relating to their flats. They varied considerably from builder to builder and some were more detailed than others.

All laid down what majorities were required for reaching decisions but surprisingly not all specified the procedures for carrying out common repairs. Several obliged the owner to join a residents' or owners' association which would be responsible for all common obligations. Usually details were given of the rules and regulations for meetings, the constitutions, and the appointment of office bearers. Sometimes these rules and procedures were left up to the association to decide.

Some conditions said that a factor had to be appointed and specified what the factor's duties were, how he should be paid and so on. Factored flats are discussed in chapters 5 to 8.

Unlike the title deeds of most older properties, the deeds of modern flats usually set out additional responsibilities about maintaining the gardens, cleaning the common entrance and staircase, and so on. In older properties owners tend simply to take their share of looking after the back courts or cleaning the stairs but in modern properties it is much more common to employ professional cleaning and gardening contractors. The conditions should specify what each owner's share of the costs are.

I've bought my council flat

Again the same general rules apply to purchasers of council flats as to any other flat buyers. The title deeds are the most important documents in determining your rights and duties towards the other owners.

But buying a council flat can be a little more complicated because the other flats tend all to be owned by the one owner and that owner is the district council who was once your landlord. This situation is rather new for many councils and not all of them have yet worked out the best way to manage property with a mixture of owners. They vary from authority to authority and so yet again we must stress the need to see the deeds relating to the property you have bought.

What will the council's deeds say?

All authorities' deeds should state your responsibility towards and access to the common parts of the building and grounds. Generally you will be responsible for your share of the costs on a pro rata basis, which means that if there are eight flats you will be liable for an eighth of the common costs. Some deeds however, split up the costs according to the rateable value of the individual flats.

The conditions will also specify how insurance is to be arranged and paid for and what restrictions there are on the property, such as not using the flat for business purposes. It is also common for a clause to make the owners responsible for a share of the cost of maintaining the gardens and back courts and to comply with any reasonable programme of external decoration.

Usually the council itself will do the work or select a contractor for the job and you will be asked to pay your share of the costs. You do as an owner have the right to ask that another contractor be used but if most of the flats are still owned by the district council your own vote won't count for very much when decisions are being reached.

In most cases this should not be a problem because the council has a vested interest in keeping the property in good order and also has the specialist workers and contractors to do the job. You also don't have the problem of a few owners holding back essential repairs because they cannot afford to pay for them. But you may have a problem other flat owners do not face in that your say in running the property will not count for very much if all the other flats are owned by the council. You will have less choice in what contractors to use, what estimate to accept and whether or not work should be done. If a council, for financial reasons, is cutting back on repairs and improvements there is very little you can do unless the repair is so serious that you have to call in the environmental health or building control department. Even in that case there could be problems because you are asking one department of the council to take action against another part of the council.

A few councils, but not many, have conditions which allow for the appointment of a factor.

Can I get a title condition changed?
It is possible to change a condition in a title deed but it is complicated and expensive. You have to make an application to the Lands Tribunal for Scotland. For more information on this you should see a solicitor or a local advice centre.

2
Getting work done

The last chapter explained some of your legal rights and duties as a flat owner but in practice knowing where you stand can be a lot more complicated. In this chapter we go through the process stage by stage when repair work needs to be done or when some of the owners want to improve the property. PEOPLE IN FACTORED FLATS SHOULD READ CHAPTER 6.

Keeping the property clean

Getting others to do their turn cleaning the stairs has probably been one of the most common sources of conflict among neighbours in blocks of flats. Nowadays, however, at least in modern property things are more sophisticated and usually the deeds of conditions specify that an outside cleaning contractor be taken on and what each owner's share of the costs should be.

Until recently, many local authorities had byelaws setting out owners' obligations about keeping the stairs and other common parts clean. These byelaws usually made it an offence not to take your turn at the common cleaning duties and people could be fined for not abiding by them. Now, however, cleaning comes under an Act of Parliament, the Civic Government (Scotland) Act 1982. The Act states that:

* each occupier has a duty to keep the common parts clean to the satisfaction of the district or island council;

* the district or island council can introduce byelaws for the cleaning of stairs, etc., for example how often they should be washed. If an individual owner fails to do so he could be fined up to £50, depending on the amount specified by the local byelaws;

* the council can also, by written notice require the owners to decorate the common entrance, stairways, etc.

This Act has only recently come into force and it is up to you to find out what, if any, byelaws your local council may have made about cleaning. The Act also says that councils must keep a register of byelaws open to public inspection.

Conditions specifying that outside cleaning contractors should be used are very common in modern flats but there is nothing to stop owners in older property getting together to hire a cleaner and share the costs. This is one of the things that an owners' association could do. Better management of your property is discussed in chapter 4.

Repairs are needed

Let's assume that the roof is leaking and causing dampness in your flat. You suspect that some slates may need replacing or that maybe the chimney heads need repointing. Perhaps you are even frightened that if it gets any worse your ceiling might fall in! In properly maintained buildings, of course, this situation is unlikely to arise. Ways of owners getting together to keep the property in good repair are discussed later in chapter 4.

Unless the repair is urgent, the first thing to do if you do not have a factor, is to tell the other owners that you want the work done, so that you can get estimates from tradesmen right away and instruct a firm to do the work.

If some of the owners prove sticky you should find out how many of you need to agree to the work and what each person's share of the cost will be. (Ideally, as a responsible owner, you will know this already.) Your title deeds will tell you what you want to know.

I can't get agreement from my neighbours

Getting agreement from everyone can be a sorry task, though it is one that is made much easier if you have a properly organised owners' association.

If the repair is urgent you will probably be able to get it done even without the consent of the other owners. Most title deeds allow for work to be instructed by one owner alone if the property is likely to deteriorate without the repair being done. This would allow you to go ahead and order the work, but it is not the end of your problems. Most tradesmen will take jobs only from an individual or from a properly organised association. If you order the work yourself you will be liable to pay his bill and then have to chase the others up for the money, perhaps even having to take them to court for their share.

Another remedy is to contact your district council. The council has power to make sure that essential repairs are done, and, if necessary, can do the work themselves and later bill the individual owners. They will intervene if the building is in serious disrepair, or if the building will get worse if the work is not done, or if a defect in one flat is likely to cause damage in another. But they can also take steps about any repair that is needed, whether it is serious or not.

The council will not force improvements on owners of a perfectly adequate property just because one or two of the owners want to make it look nicer. So, if you would like to take advantage of environmental improvement grants to landscape the back court but you can't get the agreement of the other owners, the council will not force them to do the work unless the back court is in need of repairs (for example, if the bin shed is dangerous).

The council should, however, take action over your leaky roof.

What happens when I call in the council?

Firstly a district council officer will come out to inspect the building. If he agrees that action is necessary a repairs notice will be sent to all the owners telling them that the work should be done within a certain time. At this stage most owners will probably agree to get the work done and there will be no need for the council to do it themselves.

Owners can appeal against a repairs notice. The appeal must be made to the Sheriff Court on the grounds that the repair is not necessary. This very seldom happens but if it does it can hold up the work for some time. Not having enough money is no ground for appeal. Owners in financial difficulties should read chapter 10.

If the date specified in the repairs notice has passed and the owners still have done nothing, the council can itself arrange for the job to be done (though you may have to put pressure on the council to act). Each owner will be sent a bill for their share of the work and it is up to the council to collect the money due. These shares are usually worked out according to the rateable value of each flat and so, if your title deeds divide the responsibilities differently, this is something you have to sort out yourself with your neighbours.

One advantage of getting the council in is that the council has to collect the money from each of the owners and you are saved this reponsibility. People who are reluctant to agree to having repairs done are usually also reluctant to pay their share, and trying to force money out of neighbours can be an unpleasant task. More about slow payers later in this chapter.

The main disadvantage of asking the council to do it is that the whole procedure can sometimes take months and the repairs may be more expensive than getting in a firm yourself. The council will also charge an administration fee, which is usually about 11½ per cent of the repair costs.

Contacting the council is really a last-ditch step and is no substitute for owners coming together and properly organising a system of planned maintenance and repair. (Better ways to organise repairs are discussed in chapter 4.)

Ordering the work

Assuming you now have agreement from the other owners, the main task is to get someone to do the job. Getting estimates from several firms is important, though choosing between them can be difficult. It is tempting to go always for the cheapest, but cost should not be the only criterion.

Many people have been stung by unscrupulous firms. They may offer to do the work cheaper than anyone else but then they do the job very badly. By the time you find this out and try to complain, there is no-one to complain to. The firm may have gone out of business or else it has otherwise "disappeared". There are plenty of cowboys in the building trade and, though they are disowned by the many respectable and efficient firms in the trade, they still manage to crop up again and again to exploit innocent owner-occupiers.

In one Glasgow tenement the owner-occupiers chose the contractor offering the cheapest estimate to carry out a roof repair. What they did not know was that the estimate was low because the firm was cutting corners on official health and safety regulations for its workers. The Factory Inspector ordered the contractor off the site and the roof lay half-finished for several weeks until the owners could find another contractor.

Sometimes it is hard to know exactly what the quoted price includes. One firm may say that the leaky roof will cost £300, another £450 and yet another £3,000! The firm estimating £3,000 is not necessarily trying to cheat you but may genuinely think that much more work needs to be done than you have asked for. This firm might advise you that complete re-roofing would save you money in the long term, because it will prevent other problems arising soon elsewhere on the roof. So it is worth asking for detailed written quotations so that you know exactly what work is being suggested.

Deciding between these competing claims is difficult. All you, as an owner, know is that the roof leaks and that something should be done about it. You can't be expected to know what long-term protective measures should be taken.

That's where the value of getting a specialised outside report comes in. For major jobs you could employ a surveyor or an architect or a building science expert to advise you on what is absolutely necessary, what is recommended and on possible future improvements. The surveyor will give you some idea of the costs but he will not tell you exactly how much the tradesmen should be charging for the job. Surveyors do not come cheap, and so you should use them only when a major item of expense is being considered or where you are not sure what kind of repair is needed. They are also useful in situations when the owners as a group want a complete run-down on the state of their building so that they can plan future maintenance.

Personal recommendations from other neighbours can be useful — and they come free of charge. Contact owners and owners' associations in other buildings and ask them what they think of certain contractors. They might be able to recommend firms or put you off firms they have had bad experiences with. The experiences of other owners should be as important to you as the prices the firms have quoted.

Find out whether firms are members of a trade association — they are likely to be more reputable and trustworthy.

Nevertheless, you and the other owners may try your best to get the best and cheapest firm to do the job and yet still come a cropper. What to do when the work is unsatisfactory is discussed in chapter 3.

The other owners won't pay their share

Unfortunately this is a common problem. The bills come in but some people act as if they do not exist, thinking perhaps that by forgetting about them they will go away. In some cases the owners simply cannot afford to pay their share(see Chapter 10 about how to get financial help). In other cases the owners could afford to pay but simply refuse. Negligence by the owners, be they landlords or owner-occupiers, has been one of the main reasons that so many of Scotland's tenements have gradually deteriorated and required the injection of funds from local authorities or central government to bring them up to standard. The same could happen to modern buildings, conversions and

22

council house flats which have been bought by their tenants. In most of these properties, however, a better system of organising common maintenance has been introduced from the start.

Everyone has to pay their share according to what it says in the title deeds (usually, shared equally between the owners). As a last resort you might have to take legal action against the slow payers. This might be very important if you have already paid the tradesman.

Do I have to pay the tradesman my neighbour's share of the bill?

It all depends who asked the firm to do the work. If you have a properly organised owners' association it can order the work and be billed for it as a group. The association would probably also have a fund to help with running costs and repairs so that no-one would be out of pocket if the bill was paid immediately.

If, however, you have no owners' association the firm is unlikely to accept an order from a group of people. The firm wants to make sure it will be paid for the work. But they may take an order from an individual owner. If you are that owner and some of your neighbours don't pay up you are in a very difficult position. Legally you must pay the tradesman's bills and, if you cannot get the money off the other owners, you would then have to either write the debt off or take them to court.

Legal advice at this stage would be useful. Chapter 11 explains how some owners may be entitled to free legal advice or to a reduction in the fees, if they are on low incomes and have few savings. Other sources of advice are Citizens' Advice Bureaux and local advice centres.

Think carefully before going to court. If you lose you usually have to pay not only your own legal costs but also those of the neighbours you are suing. If you win it could still take further action and some time before you get your money back and there will be a lot of ill-feeling.

You do not have to use a lawyer to go to court, though doing without one is not easy. If you are thinking of doing without a lawyer you should get advice about this from a local advice centre.

REMEMBER THAT IF YOU HAVE ORDERED THE JOB YOURSELF YOU CANNOT GET OUT OF PAYING THE WHOLE BILL JUST BECAUSE THE OTHER OWNERS REFUSE TO PAY THEIR SHARE.

3
Unsatisfactory work

You and the other owners may have tried your hardest to get the best and cheapest firm and yet still come a cropper. What do you do if the work is not up to scratch?

Every customer has the right to expect that tradesmen will use a reasonable standard of skill. So, if your leaky roof starts leaking again in the same place the work was probably faulty. But things are more complicated than that. Perhaps the roof repairs are carried out adequately but another leak starts elsewhere on the roof. Unless you had asked for a complete roof overhaul you would have no legal remedy against the firm which carried out the stop-gap repairs you ordered.

If the job you specified is done badly you should be entitled to compensation. In most cases you should at least get a reduction in the bill but if the job was so badly botched that you had to get someone else in to do it you should not have to pay for the work that was badly done.

Occasionally a firm might even have to give you extra compensation if they made such a mess of the job that further damage was caused. For example, if the tradesmen damaged the gutters while repairing the roof the firm should pay you the extra cost of getting the gutters replaced.

In most cases, however, the work is just not up to standard and all you want the firm to do is come and finish the job off properly.

YOU SHOULD CHECK THE REPAIR WORK AS SOON AS POSSIBLE AFTER COMPLETION.

We haven't yet paid the bill and don't intend to!

If the bill hasn't yet been paid you are obviously in a stronger negotiating position. The firm has to chase you for the money rather than you going to great lengths to get back what you have

already paid. But you should remember that at the end of the day you will have to pay for the work that has been properly done.

Normally what you should do is write to the firm as early as possible complaining about the work, stating exactly what is wrong with it and what you want done about it. The letter should be dated and you should keep a copy.

Your letter should clearly state what it is that you want. It is also useful to give a time limit in which you want to receive the firm's reply. After that several things could happen.

* The firm may ignore your letter, in which case you can either write to them again, this time through your solicitor, or sit tight and wait for them to chase you up for the money. Although you have not yet paid the bill, sitting tight is not always the wisest course of action, unless the defects in the work are very slight. If the work has been so badly done that it could affect your living standards or could make the property deteriorate even more, you will want to get someone else out to do it as soon as possible or else get the original firm back to finish the job properly.

* They may write back offering to do the job properly. You don't have to accept their offer if you would rather employ someone else but, if you do agree, this does not affect your legal rights later if the work is still not done properly. You certainly should not be charged more for the firm to come back, unless you are now asking them to do more than you originally asked them to do. This does sometimes happen. Sometimes owners go for the cheapest option and ask the tradesman to do only stop-gap repairs. It is not his fault if these repairs are not enough to prevent further damage. A good firm, however, should have told you before what work is necessary. Nevertheless, the firm does not have a duty to advise you on other repairs and is responsible only for the work you instructed them to do.

* The firm could write refusing either to come back to finish the job or to accept any reduction in fees. Such a letter usually includes a reminder that the money is now due and if not paid they will take legal action against you. In this case you have to brace yourself for the fact that you could be sued by the firm for the money.

Whatever the firm's answer, or if there is no answer at all, you have to discuss with your neighbours what your next course of action should be.

If the firm is a member of a trade association check whether or not the association has an arbitration service you can use. Another tactic might be to get an expert report to send to the firm. These professional reports are done usually by surveyors, architects, clerks of works, building science lecturers at a college or university, or sometimes by other builders. You should expect to pay a fee for the report. Names of surveyors, architects and other builders can be found in your local Yellow Pages telephone book. Your solicitor or an advice agency should also be able to recommend someone.

You also have to decide whether or not to go to court. Going to court takes time and if you lose it could cost you money as well. It is always a last resort.

In the meantime the next step is yet another letter to the firm either from yourselves or from a solicitor. This is a good time to get legal advice. One of your neighbours might be able to get this free under the Legal Advice and assistance scheme. See chapter 10.

Other sources of advice at this stage include Citizens' Advice Bureaux and other advice agencies, although they are unlikely to be able to represent you in court if the need arises.

The firm is taking us to court

If, despite your letters, the firm does decide to take you to court over the bill you must think carefully before deciding to fight it to the bitter end. Your solicitor will be able to advise you on how sound your case is, but if you do lose the case you will have to pay not only the original bill but also the firm's legal expenses as well as your own. Ask your solicitor in advance how much it is likely to cost you.

You do not have to use a solicitor. You can defend yourselves in court if you want to but this is more difficult than it sounds.

In any case, you have to make sure that your case is as watertight as possible. Take photographs of the repairs/damage, using a professional photographer if you can afford one. Get a building expert to inspect the work and give you a written report on it. You could also call on the expert to give verbal evidence for you in court.

What can the court decide?

If you do have to go to court the Sheriff can decide either that:
You were not justified in refusing to pay the bill. In this case you will be ordered to pay the money by a certain date, usually by fixed instalments. You will also have to pay the firm's legal costs as well as your own.

or that:

You were justified in not paying the bill because the work you instructed was not done satisfactorily and with a reasonable degree of skill. In this case the Sheriff would either decide that you should pay only a certain part of the bill or that you should pay nothing at all. He will usually also order the firm to pay your legal costs.

In this situation, since you are defending a case brought by the firm, the Sheriff is not allowed to award you extra compensation for any damage caused by the firm which might have involved you in extra expenditure. For this you would have to take a separate legal action.

I paid the bill before I noticed the work was faulty

In many cases the fault is not discovered until after you have paid the bill. How do you get your money back?

To start with the procedure is the same as if you had not yet paid the bill. Write a letter (and keep a copy) to the firm explaining exactly what you think is wrong with the work and what you want them to do about it. Explain whether you want them to come back and do the job properly, whether you are asking for return of some of the money, or whether you want them to give you back all of the money. In some cases you might want more than your money back. For example, if the tradesmen broke windows on the half landing while they were swinging their ladders onto the roof, you should claim for the extra cost of getting new panes of glass put in.

Discuss carefully with the other owners what realistically you want to achieve and the best way to get it. You need not accept the firm's offer to repair the damage if you do not want to, and in some cases the last thing you would want is for the same incompetent tradesmen to appear on your doorstep. But in most cases an offer to repair the damage properly would be acceptable, provided that the work is done quickly. Accepting such an offer does not jeopardise your legal rights later to go to court if the work is still not up to scratch.

The firm which refuses to do anything at all causes the most headaches because in that case you may have little choice but to go to court. Again, you and your neighbours must think out your strategy carefully. If you can afford to, get legal advice. Remember that some owners may be entitled to free legal advice and assistance if they are on low incomes. Alternatively, get advice from a Citizens' Advice Bureau or from another advice agency.

At this stage the situation is very similar to what you would do if you had not already paid the bill, though in this case there could be more urgency because you have already paid out your own hard-earned cash. The firm might ignore your letter, in which case you should write to them again, perhaps through your solicitor. The firm might reply denying any liability and refusing either to come back and do the job properly or to give you some of your money back. They might deny any responsibility at all for damage caused by them while they were on the job.

It is remarkable what can sometimes be achieved if you write again sharply threatening to take legal action, preferably through a solicitor. Often the firm will come back with an offer to have another look at the work to bring it up to standard. Seldom do they at this stage offer a reduction in their charges. In either case you do not have to accept their offer if it is not what you want. But be reasonable. They know, as you should know too, that going to court is no guarantee of success and that empty threats deserve to be treated as such.

Before deciding to go ahead with court action you might think it worthwhile to get some kind of expert report done on the property and on the standard of repairs. As explained earlier, inspections and reports can be done by a surveyor, an architect, a clerk of works, a building science expert or another builder. Normally you will be charged a fee for the written report but it would be money well spent if you win the case, especially as this would be one of the expenses you would charge to the contractor. Photographs of the work are also useful, preferably using a professional photographer.

Let us assume that you and the other owners have decided to go ahead with court action because you think you have a good case. What kind of action do you have to take? There is a difference between you and the owner who has not yet paid the bill. You will be initiating legal action against the contractor, instead of merely defending an action by the firm for payment of their account.

You would have to take an action for damages against the firm. This means that you are claiming compensation for any loss you have suffered. You could seek return of some of the money you have paid or, if the defects in the job were major and you had to employ someone else to do the job, all your money back. In some cases you might claim back more than you paid in the original bill, for example if the contractor had damaged other parts of the building causing you even more expense or if the work was so badly done that it cost you more to get a reputable firm in to do the job from start to finish.

That is what you can do legally, but before embarking on such an exercise it is worth finding out about the cost. If you win you usually have to pay no costs at all, but if you lose you could end up paying the contractor's legal costs as well as your own. Should you use a solicitor? In most cases it is advisable to use a solicitor even though it is possible to do it yourself.

Can we sue the firm as a group of owners?

This is where the problems come in. There is no such thing in Scotland as court actions being taken by a group of people. They must be taken either by certain kinds of organisations, such as companies or partnerships, or by individuals themselves. Unless your owners' association has formed itself into a company or partnership, there is no way that you can take a court action together against the contractor. Unfortunately each of you must take legal action individually.

That could mean up to twelve different court actions against the same contractor. In some ways this is a good thing because it shows that you are all united in your action and if the first case to be heard is successful the others are likely to follow suit. But it also means a lot of legal fees if you lose.

If some of the owners are entitled to legal aid it might be better for only those owners to take court action. If they win, the firm will probably concede defeat to the other owners, but if the firm refuses to do this at least you know that the rest of you are likely to be successful when you take your cases to court. As explained earlier, you will be able to recover most of your legal costs if you win the case.

If the work was ordered by one owner he is legally liable for the bill and has to take the court action himself. In this case co-operation between all the owners is crucial. It is unfair to make one owner the scapegoat. The other owners should get together a fund to pay for legal costs if he loses. If the owners are properly organised this should never happen.

The work is taking too long

This is a common complaint. Sometimes contractors take much longer on a job than you were initially led to believe and longer than you think is reasonable. It is sensible when you hire the firm to ask them how long it will take to do the job, because time is sometimes just as important as price.

If the work has not yet started and you have waited an unreasonably long time you are free to cancel the agreement with the firm and ask another firm to do the work for you instead. You should write to the firm and ask them to complete the work within a certain time. State that if the work is not done in that time you will treat the contract as cancelled and go elsewhere. In these cases be careful, because a second firm might not be able to start work right away either.

If, however, work has already started and it is still dragging on the situation is more complicated. The contractor is not in breach of contract unless he specified a time limit with you beforehand. In most cases some pressure from the owners will spur the firm into more activity but if that does not work you may have to think about getting another firm in to finish the job. Think carefully before doing this for several reasons:

*   the original firm may have come up against complications which they did not anticipate and which could genuinely have held up their progress;

*   it might not be easy to get another firm to take on the job and finish it off more quickly than the present contractor;

*   it might cost you more money if you have to change to another firm.

Again you should write to the firm asking them to complete the work within a certain period and state that you will treat the contract as cancelled if the work is not done by then.

If you switch contracts in the middle of the job you will be liable for the original's firm's costs as well as the costs of the new contractor. On the other hand, if the firm has taken an unjustifiably long time to complete a job the contractor could well be liable to pay you damages for your losses, especially if extra costs have been incurred because the building has deteriorated in the meantime.

Time is not usually regarded as of the essence of a contract but if the delay is unusually long and has cost you extra money you could be entitled to some compensation. See a solicitor or advice agency about this.

Factored flats

If you live in a factored flat the factor will probably be able to negotiate with the firm for you and employ a solicitor if you have to go to court. But the factor will charge you for this. People who are unhappy with the work that a factor has ordered should read chapter 6.

4
Managing your property better

The usual haphazard way in which individual owners organise repairs is not always effective. If you really want to keep your property in good condition and avoid problems in the future you must get some kind of system going. The options are either to get yourselves together into an association, either formally or informally, or to use a factor. Factoring is discussed in chapters 5 to 8.

The first step

Unfortunately the first time people get together tends to be when a substantial repair needs done. It is much better to get organised BEFORE urgent repairs are necessary.

Ask your neighbours to come to a meeting to talk about the property. It should not be very formal; a chat over a cup of coffee in your living room would be enough. This may even be the first time you have really spoken to some of your neighbours. Don't be put off if few people turn up. People are busy with their own lives and might not feel that a neighbours' meeting is very important. In many cases there is one person who does all the organising and the others are quite happy to leave everything up to that one person.

It is pretty pointless arranging the meeting yourself and then going round to tell everyone about it. Find out what time suits most people best and try to get a date and time that suits as many of your neighbours as possible. If there is a housebound person in the property or a single parent who can't get a babysitter it might be better to hold the meeting in her house rather than in your own. If there are rented flats in your block you should invite both landlords and tenants.

You cannot expect too much of the first meeting, but it is at least a chance to get to know your neighbours and find out what complaints they have. Their complaints may be about the way repairs have been done in the past or how much money it has cost them, they may be about some particular repair that is affecting them more than others in the stair, or they could even be about the other owners, especially if one owner is a property firm rather than an owner-occupier. Take a note not only of the complaints but also of what improvements people would like to see done, such as cleaning up the back court or repainting the stair walls.

An Owners' Association

It is all very well getting together and agreeing on what repairs or improvements need to be done but you might still face problems if you do not decide how to organise these repairs. Informal get-togethers are very useful but they cannot replace a properly organised system of maintaining the property.

The best thing to do is to form an owners' association. ALL the owners should agree to this and so the interested owners might have a lot of persuading to do to get anything off the ground. In the meantime, get in touch with other groups of owners to find out what kind of association they have set up. If you do not know anyone else who is in an owners' or residents' association, contact your local Council for Social Service which can put you in touch with other groups. Contact the Scottish Council for Social Services in Edinburgh for the address and telephone number of your nearest local Council.

The association should have a constitution. This should state that all owners in the building or in the close should be members, when the annual general meeting will be held, how often other meetings will be held, and how decisions are to be made. Normally decisions should be reached on the basis of one household one vote.

If you do get agreement from all the other owners to set up an owners' association you will be in a good position to make sure that work is not held back by some owners. Decisions of the association would normally be reached by majority so that, even if your title deeds specify that all owners have to agree to work

being done, you would be able to instruct work on agreement of a majority of the owners, PROVIDED THAT ALL OWNERS ARE MEMBERS OF THE ASSOCIATION.

Legal advice from a solicitor is very useful at this stage so that you are sure your constitution means exactly what you all want it to mean. Other residents' associations can also pinpoint pitfalls you might not have thought of.

Your association will need a treasurer and a secretary. The treasurer is absolutely vital — someone has to look after the money. But a secretary is also useful to deal with correspondence, take complaints, get estimates and order work in an emergency. Firms prefer to deal with one person rather than with lots of different people. It is not so necessary to elect a chairperson (though most associations do) because you can all take turns chairing the meetings if you prefer.

Paying the bills

The first thing the treasurer should do is open a bank account in the name of the association. Usually at least two people have to sign if money is being withdrawn or cheques written. This should be agreed with the bank in advance. You might prefer to have a deposit account so that interest builds up on your money, but a current account is also useful for signing cheques and dealing with day to day business.

There is little point in going to all the bother of getting an association going if the same old problems are going to crop up again and again over repair bills. What most associations do is fix a membership fee for all owners. This covers the cost of stamps and stationery that the secretary will use up writing to tradesmen or to the district council and any other expenses incurred by the association. It is sensible to keep the membership subscription as low as possible and to collect it once a year.

A repairs and maintenance fund is also a good idea. Repairs bills can drop through the letterbox with horrifying regularity and, unless there is some cash already in the bank, some owners can face huge problems trying to meet their share. It is better to spread these costs throughout the year. If each owner pays in a regular weekly or monthly sum to the association's repairs fund, there will always be money to cope with urgent repairs. And if no repairs need to be done that year the money still collects interest from the bank.

How much each person should pay is up to the association. You want to make sure that the payments are high enough to meet most repairs bills but if you make the monthly payments too high some people will be put off and refuse to pay. Some properties will need bigger repairs funds than others, especially if the property is old and a lot of work needs to be done. What must be understood by all members of the association is that if a major repair is needed the fund might not be enough to pay for it and in that case everyone will still have to put their hands in their pockets for their share of the bill.

A programme of planned maintenance

Patching-up operations may seem cheap at the time, but eventually you might have to do something more serious — and expensive — to deal with the problem. A neglected roof which has had occasional minor repairs could one day collapse. An outbreak of dry rot will not go away if you ignore it — in fact it will very quickly spread to other areas.

Instead of dealing with each problem as it arises the association should find out what needs to be done to prolong the future of the property. Regular maintenance is cheaper in the long term than a series of stop-gap repairs.

A useful start for the association is to get a full structural survey done by a qualified surveyor. It will cost you money but at least you will know what state the building is in and what needs to be done to it. After that you can work out your priorities and decide what you can as an association afford to do now and what you will have to hold back until later. Obviously urgent repairs should be done right away but there may also be improvements that you want to do which can be held back until there is more money in the account. You don't have to do everything at once.

It is worthwhile finding out about council grants and loans that might be available for certain repairs and improvements. Chapter 10 explains these in more detail.

Finally, a programme of planned maintenance means that you should all be aware of what might be needed in the future as well as at the moment. Your roof might be in good condition now but in five years it might need a lot of work done on it. It is important to work out a timetable for regular checks on the property. You do not need a full structural survey every year but you should make some arrangements for the building to be inspected at least once every few years. Why wait until the top-floor owners' ceiling falls down and the repair costs perhaps thousands of pounds — when a cheaper roof repair done a few years earlier could have saved both money and hardship?

5
Factored flats

A large proportion of the flats in Glasgow and the West of Scotland have factors who look after the repair and maintenance of the property. The word "factor" may mean very little to people in other parts of the country or, if it does, it usually suggests some kind of landlord's agent in eighteenth-century rural Scotland. Even those owners with factors, however, are sometimes confused about their legal relationship with him.

The factor is, quite simply, an agent of the owners. He has certain duties and powers, mainly about the insurance, repair and maintenance of the property, but he is answerable to the individual owners who pay for his services, be they owner-occupiers or landlords. In theory flat owners elsewhere could benefit a lot from the "Glasgow" factoring system but in practice there are a lot of complaints about the way factors operate. Many of these complaints arise because the owners themselves do not understand the factor's role.

The historical background

Most tenements were built towards the end of the nineteenth century and were bought by landlords as an investment. To collect rents from the tenants they employed factors. The factors also saw to the repair and maintenance of the properties and acted as the landlords' agents. In Edinburgh landlords usually used solicitors but in Glasgow they used firms which specialised in this kind of work.

Since the First World War more and more tenement flats have been sold by landlords to individual owner-occupiers. Most of them have now changed hands several times but the factor who once worked for the landlord now works for all the owners in the stair. There are still many tenement stairs where some flats are owned by owner-occupiers and others by landlords. In these cases the landlord owns no more than his normal share of the common parts of the building and the factor is as much an agent of the owner-occupiers as of the big landlord firms. But confusion has sometimes arisen because the factor has this dual role of rent collector and agent of the new owners.

As a landlord's agent the factor had more freedom to take decisions than as the agent of owner-occupiers concerned only about maintaining their own property. He would collect rents and use the money as a float for any repairs that were necessary. He would take all the day-to-day decisions on the owner's behalf and, in fact, many tenants did not even know who the owner was. Some tenants believed that the factor was the owner of the property because the factor was the only person they dealt with. Occasionally the factor was also the owner.

Common complaints about factors

The Scottish Consumer Council a few years ago asked the public for information about factoring and received a surprisingly high number of complaints. Not all of them were in fact the fault of the factor, but the sheer level of response indicated that there is a lot of dissatisfaction about the way factoring works for owner-occupiers.

"The job wasn't done properly".
"We had the roof fixed last month but it's still leaking".
"Our factor never comes to see the building".
"We never get to see estimates".
"We were sure that no work had been done on the roof all year, but we were charged for repairs on it".
"The factor keeps using the same firms even though they don't do the job properly".

These are typical of the kind of complaints we received about factors. Broadly they fall into five main categories.

* The poor quality of the work arranged by the factor.

* The cost of the work and fears that the factor uses his building trade contacts instead of getting the best and cheapest firm to do the work.

* Lack of consultation with the owners about what work needs to be done and what tradesmen are to be used.

* Fears that the owners are being charged for work that has never been done.

* Criticisms of other owners who hold up maintenance work for months because they refuse to agree to it, or because they are so slow in paying up that the factor is reluctant to get a major repair done.

Factors also have complaints about owners. In some cases the factor's reluctance to instruct repairs is because he knows how difficult it will be to get money from some of the owners.

The factor's powers

The factor's powers and duties may be laid down in the title deeds to the property and are also governed by the common law of agency. See chapter 1 for more detail on title deeds and how to get hold of them. Normally he can make decisions on behalf of all the owners as if the owners had got together and agreed at a meeting. The factor is employed to decide what work needs to be done and which firm should do it.

He is there to save the owners a lot of time and trouble. Legally he is your agent and you have given him power to make decisions on your behalf. He is not obliged to consult with the owners beforehand. If, for example, the guttering needs replaced and the factor has instructed Ham Fisted Ltd to do the work you cannot complain afterwards that he should have used Super Efficient Builders Ltd instead because they would have done the job more cheaply.

In most cases the factor does consult the owners before embarking on a major repair, but he is not obliged to do so. Problems with the factor are discussed more fully in the next few chapters.

The Model Conditions

Concerned about the problems between owners and factors, the Property Owners and Factors Association of Glasgow a few years ago drew up what they call ''Model Conditions of Management of Premises in Flatted Property''. Most flat owners who have a factor will by now have seen a copy and been asked to sign it.

The Association believes that it has been a serious handicap for both owners and factors that until now there was little written down about their powers and duties apart from what was in the title deeds. Their Model Conditions include a number of rules and a list of the factor's duties. For some duties the factor may charge an extra fee.

Certainly any attempt to clarify in more detail the relationship between owner and factor is to be welcomed but you do not have to accept the one drawn up by the Property Owners and Factors Association. In some flatted properties in Glasgow the Model Conditions have already been accepted by the owners. If you have not already signed it you are free to suggest changes in the agreement. The Scottish Consumer Council hopes this booklet will help you work out which conditions are suited to you and which are not. In any case some sort of agreement between the owners and the factor is well advised because of the problems that can crop up.

Such a contract between owners and factor must be made with the agreement of the other owners. You as an individual cannot reach agreement with the factor about his powers and duties towards the other owners. In most cases a simple majority of the owners is enough and this will bind the other owners to the agreement, but in some properties ALL owners have to agree. Only your title deeds can clarify this, so see chapter 1 on how to get hold of your title deeds.

If you cannot reach agreement with the factor about the terms of his work, you will have to decide one of three options:

* accept the factor's terms so that he will continue working for you;

* find a new factor who is prepared to work on your terms;

* manage your property without a factor.

Dismissing factors is explained later in this chapter. Those who wish to manage their own property without a factor should read chapters 2, 3 and 4.

Even if you have already signed the Model Conditions, this does not prevent you from renegotiating certain terms in it. The owners should first work out together what changes they want made so that they can approach the factor as a united group. If, after discussion, the factor is not prepared to budge you must decide among yourselves whether to continue using him on the old terms or to dismiss him and find another way of managing the property.

A copy of the Model Conditions is in the Appendix, but throughout the chapters which follow we shall also refer to various relevant parts of the Model Conditions.

Do I have to have a factor?

There is no need to have a factor if the owners do not want one. If you all agree to dismiss the factor it is your right as owners to do so. In many cases, depending on what the title deeds say (see chapter 1), it is enough for a majority of the owners to agree to dismiss the factor and either employ another firm or organise the repairs and maintenance themselves.

Occasionally the deeds say that a factor MUST be appointed and may even name the factor. The original owner of the property will have laid down this condition but you are not bound by it PROVIDED THAT ALL OF THE OWNERS agree to changing the factor or not using one at all.

Should we get rid of our factor?

Dismissing your factor is usually very straightforward, but think carefully before deciding on this course of action. Factors do save the owners a lot of effort and there are ways of making the arrangement between factors and owners work better. Doing it all yourselves can be time-consuming, costly and bitter, especially if some of your neighbours are not too keen on paying for their share of the work.

Chapters 2 and 3 describe some of the pitfalls faced by owners without a factor and chapter 4 suggests some ways of getting the owners organised successfully without using a factor. After reading them you might decide that having a factor is the easiest way of maintaining the property. In many cases there is no need to dismiss the factor at all if you can reach agreement with him about a better way to manage the property. Chapter 8 has a checklist of the pros and cons of factoring.

How do we dismiss the factor?

The first thing to do is talk with other owners about your common problems. Then approach the factor with your requirements. If, after discussion, he is still not amenable you might have to change the factor. Remember that other factors may demand the same terms as the factor you are using now.

The title deeds usually say that a simple majority of the owners is enough to dismiss the factor but in some cases the consent of all owners is required. This can cause difficulties if some of the flats are still owned by private landlords or even by the factor himself.

In some cases the deeds say that one particular owner should decide who the factor is. In this situation the owner may be swayed by evidence of bad management by the factor. After all, it is in his interests to keep the property in good condition.

If the owners agree to dismiss the factor the rest is straight-forward. One of the owners should write a letter signed by all the owners ending the agreement with the factor and stating from what date this takes effect. Dismissing the factor does not mean that you can get out of paying any money already owed to him. So be prepared to clear your debts with the factor either when you stop using him or shortly afterwards.

The same rules apply to appointing a new factor. Depending on the title deeds, either a majority of the owners or all the owners need to agree on whom to use. Factoring firms have close contacts with each other and so if you leave one firm with large debts you could find difficulties getting another factor to take you on. Similarly, you will find that the terms factors are willing to work under do not vary much from firm to firm.

Factors and owners — the fundamentals

* YOU are the owner of your own flat and also of your share in the common parts of the building. It is YOUR responsibility to keep the property in good repair.

* The factor is your agent and can take decisions on your behalf, but it is open to you to renegotiate the agreement between factor and owners if you are dissatisfied with it and, as a last resort, to remove the factor.

* The factor is there to provide a service which you pay for. You should expect value for money.

The next three chapters outline the kind of service you should expect from your factor and what remedies you have if you are dissatisfied.

6
The factor and repairs

The factor has the right to instruct repairs on behalf of the owners without going to them for permission first. That does not mean, however, that he is legally responsible for ensuring that the property is in good condition. He has no obligation to inspect the property regularly to find out what repairs and improvements are necessary.

The best way of ensuring that repairs are done regularly is for the owners to organise themselves into a group and arrange a programme of planned maintenance. This is discussed more fully in chapter 8. The Model Conditions of the Property Owners and Factors Association, referred to in the last chapter, do have a clause stating that one of the duties of the factor is to make regular visits to the property. If you have agreed to the Model Conditions, or if you have managed to negotiate some other kind of written agreement with the factor, it is up to you to decide with the factor how often you want the building inspected. Even so, he is still your agent and you have no legal comeback on him if he fails to notice essential repairs that need done. The duty to detect damage to the building is yours.

Through his years of experience in the business the factor should be able to notice faults more easily than can the average owner-occupier but if he does not do so there is little you can do about it except change your factor. In all fairness to the factor he may not have the skills of a surveyor or builder and, unless you have specifically asked him to get full structural surveys done on the property, you cannot expect him to detect all faults in the building.

Getting work done

In most cases the factor instructs work, not as a result of a routine check on the building, but because an individual owner-occupier has made a complaint. In that case he DOES have a duty

to act on the complaint, if necessary by making a visit to the building before instructing a tradesman.

A fairly common criticism is that there are long delays before work is started after the complaint is made. It takes time to get estimates and make sure that the firm is free to do the job as soon as possible, but one of the advantages of using a factor is supposed to be that he has good contacts with builders and can get work done faster. If there seems to be an unnecessary delay, the owners should contact the factor to find out why.

With large expensive repairs there may be an even greater delay because the factor will usually try to get agreement from all the owners before he orders the work. This is partly in his own interests — he does not want to be left with large bills that the owners will not pay. It is also in the interests of the owners. If you believe that you should have a say in what tradesmen to use and how much to spend on the work, you must expect to spend some time looking at estimates before the work can start.

Small jobs

Most small jobs will be organised by the factor without consulting the owners. That is, after all, what you are paying him for. If you insist on seeing every estimate for every small job your factor is likely to get fed up and give up on you. In any case it would lead to even more delays in getting the work done.

So, if a small repair needs to be done the factor will go straight ahead and some owners may not even know about the job until the factor's bill comes in. You must pay your share of the cost, whether you knew about the work or not. Later in this chapter we discuss what to do if the work is unsatisfactory.

I want to be consulted over large jobs

It can be a shock to get the factor's bill and discover that he has spent thousands of pounds for you that you did not even know about! Fortunately most factors get agreement from the owners first if they know the repair is going to be a large one. But the factor is not obliged to do this unless your agreement with him says you must be consulted.

The Model Conditions say that the owners should be consulted over expensive jobs. It is up to you and the factor to fix a figure for what is expensive and what is not. The dividing line may be somewhere between £150 and £250, but you can ask for a higher or lower figure if you want.

Do not set the amount too low or you could end up spending a lot of time over every little job that needs done and the factor's administrative costs could be higher (paid for by you in the management fee). But if you set it too high you will have little say on what firms are used except for very expensive jobs.

With big jobs the factor may also ask each owner to pay part of the cost in advance. This is discussed later in the chapter.

The other owners won't agree

The factor will not normally go ahead with large repairs until he has the agreement of at least a majority of owners in the stair. Getting agreement can be a slow process. The factor will write to each owner describing the job and enclosing at least one estimate. But some owners are slow to respond to letters like this. Some may hope that if they don't reply nothing will be done and they will be saved money.

Sticky owners like that really make life difficult for the factor and for the other owners. They are often the cause of delays that are blamed on the factor.

"We first heard from the people on the top floor that they had asked the factor to do something about the roof. A few weeks later we received a letter asking us to agree to an estimate and to send in a £50 deposit towards the cost. I did this and nothing happened for months. Eventually we were sent a new estimate because prices had gone up."

This complaint is typical of many others and it is easy to blame the factor for the delay. In many cases, however, it is one of the owners who has held up the job by not replying to the factor's letter.

Factors could do more to get agreement from the owners. Some hold owners' meetings and this often speeds things up. People have the chance to ask questions, express their fears and discuss what needs to be done. If some owners are proving difficult you should ask the factor to organise a meeting or arrange one yourself with the other owners. This is good practice anyway and is discussed in chapter 8.

It is important for flat owners to understand that putting off big repairs is more expensive in the long term. No-one is ever happy paying out large bills, especially if you are not directly affected by the fault. You may not be inconvenienced by a leaking roof if you live on the ground floor but eventually if repairs are not done the roof will get worse and the building deteriorate. Unrepaired roofs lead to dampness which can cause rot which could spread to YOUR flat. And if you later want to sell, you could find it more difficult. Building societies will not lend on buildings in a bad state of repair — however nicely you have done up your own flat. Also the value of your flat will decrease if the building needs repaired.

If, however, you can't get the other owners to agree to the work the factor will probably go ahead with a small repair instead. But constant patching is no substitute for a thorough overhaul and repair. A series of cheap small repairs may solve the immediate problem but may turn out to be a bad buy in the long term.

Should I call in the council?

As a last resort you might have to ask the district council to force the other owners to take action. The council has power to make sure that essential repairs are done and, if necessary, can do the work themselves and later bill the individual owners. They will intervene if the building is in serious disrepair, or if it will get worse if the work is not done, or if a defect in one flat is likely to cause damage in another flat. They can take steps for any repair that is needed but they are not likely to do so unless the fault is serious.

The biggest snag is that the council may not order a complete overhaul of the property and may insist only on what is necessary. Your factor may already be doing stop-gap repairs and the problem is not that nothing is being done but that, because some owners refuse to agree to large bills, not enough is being done to protect the future life of the building. If the factor is doing nothing at all you have three options:

* Dismiss the factor and appoint a new factor. If the problem is that some owners refuse to agree to repairs the same problem will be faced by the new factor.

* Dismiss the factor and organise the work yourselves. Again this will not solve the problem if some owners refuse to co-operate.

* Get the council in to force the other owners to do the work. (See page 18 about what happens when you call in the council).

How many estimates should I get?

Let us assume that there are no problems getting the owners to agree to the work or, if there were problems, these have now been resolved. Your next step is deciding whether or not to accept the estimate the factor has sent you for the work.

There are many complaints from owners that the factor always uses the same firm and that the owners are not convinced it is the cheapest and the best. Sometimes this is true but you must also bear in mind that the factor has building trade contacts and will know from experience what the various firms are like. If he uses the same firm regularly it might be because he can get the work done faster.

Even so, for large jobs you should see at least two estimates, and you can if you and the other owners insist on this.

The Model Conditions, which you may already have signed, say that the factor should submit "an estimate or estimates" for large jobs and that, where he considers it to be in the interests of the owners, he should get estimates from several tradesmen. This sounds as if it is up to the factor to decide how many estimates you should see!

As explained earlier, the Model Conditions can be changed by negotiation between factor and owners. One of the changes you might like to see would be that at least two estimates should be provided for large jobs. Most factors would be quite happy to agree to this.

Even if you have not signed any special agreement with your factor you can still refuse to go ahead with the work without seeing more than one estimate. We have heard of cases where the factor has refused to provide a second estimate and the owners have refused to get the work done without one. The result is deadlock and the repair continues unattended. That is an appalling situation and is the result of poor communication between factor and owners. If you do get into this situation you should discuss it as amicably as possible with the factor and try to negotiate an agreement with him.

Choosing between estimates

Choosing between estimates is very difficult and you should take account of the factor's advice. He knows that the cheapest is not always the best.

There are plenty of cowboys in the building trade and, though they are disowned by the many respectable firms in the trade, they still manage to crop up again and again to exploit innocent owner-occupiers. Some firms may be cheap because they break the official health and safety regulations for their workers. Others may do poor quality work and when you come to complain afterwards you find that the firm may have gone out of business. Problems can arise for the factor if the firm does not produce official tax certificates, which were introduced to stop tax evasion in the building industry.

It would be foolish to ignore the factor's advice altogether. Being in the business he might know which firms are better than others. On the other hand, the decision is yours.

The factor may try to argue in favour of one firm because he has always used that firm. There are advantages in putting a lot of work in the way of one firm. Firstly, the factor is in a strong negotiating position if the work is unsatisfactory because the firm will not want to lose his custom. Secondly, the firm might be prepared to do the job at short notice if you are a regular customer.

If, however, you are dissatisfied with the work done by the firm he has been using you should consider employing another firm this time.

We want to get our own estimates

Sometimes owners get their own estimates if they are unhappy with the estimates provided by the factor. Is the factor entitled to refuse to use the firm you got the estimate from?

He can do so but if he refuses you should ask him to come to a meeting to explain his reasons. It may be that he knows the firm is not a good one even though it is cheaper than the firm he recommends.

After hearing the factor's arguments it is up to the owners to decide what to do. They may decide to accept the factor's advice after all. Or they may decide to order the job themselves using their chosen tradesman. In that case they should tell the firm that the instructions come from them and not the factor.

We are fed up instructing our own work

If you find that you repeatedly have to instruct the work yourselves you would probably be better off changing your factor or not using one at all. There is little point in paying a factor's management fee if you are doing most of the management yourselves. In one case in Glasgow the owner-occupiers reached this stage without deliberately planning it.

They told us: "In the past five years all the owners decided that repairs and improvements to our property were to be done by ourselves and we feel this has saved us quite a bit of money. Although this is the case we still have to pay the factor's bills. They collect feu duties and insurance premiums on the property plus of course the management fee. What we want to know is whether we can do away with the factor altogether and factor our own property, which we feel we are doing anyway."

These owners are obviously quite successfully managing to organise their own repairs and maintenance and they do not need a factor. As explained earlier, they can dismiss him if they want to. Those who do want to go it alone should read chapters 3, 4 and 5.

The factor wants an advance payment

Requests for advance payments before a job is done are very unpopular, but from the factor's viewpoint this may be the only way he can be sure he will get the money to pay the bill when it comes in. "Floats" (discussed in chapter 8) help factors overcome to some extent their cashflow problem but the float might not be large enough to cover the costs of large repairs.

The idea of getting an advance payment from the owners is not an unreasonable one and is part of the Model Conditions, which you may have signed. But if the factor should not be out of pocket neither should the owners. We recommend that the money should be put into a deposit account and any interest on it returned to the owners. The Factors' Association has argued that this would be administratively difficult, but we think these problems could be overcome and that it is only fair for the owners rather than the factor to get interest on advance payments, especially if there is going to be a long delay before the work is done.

Ask the factor not to hand over all the money to the tradesman until the work is done and has been inspected. Holding back payment can be an effective way of forcing a firm to come back and finish unsatisfactory work. If you have already paid, it is much more difficult to get your money back.

The work is unsatisfactory

You are the one who is paying the bills and you have a right to expect the firm to do the job you asked it to do. You should also expect that a reasonable standard of skill will be used.

Depending on how botched the job was you have a right to compensation. You may be entitled to your money back or at least a reduction in price. In many cases all you want the firm to do is come back and finish the job properly — at no extra cost! Occasionally the work is so badly done that the firm might even owe you more than your money back. This would apply, for example, if the tradesmen so seriously damaged the roof when they were carrying out minor repairs that you had to get another firm in to repair the damage.

You are in a much stronger bargaining position if the factor has not already paid the bill. It is a good idea to arrange with the factor beforehand that he does not pay any bills until he has inspected the work. Sometimes, however, faults are not noticed until long after the bills have been paid.

What to do if you are dissatisfied with the work

Complain to the factor. He instructed the firm to do the job and is in a strong bargaining position to negotiate with them. The factor is likely to be even more successful on your behalf if he uses the firm regularly. They won't want to lose his custom.

Be sure, however, that your complaint is justified. The firm is only responsible for the job that you asked them to do. If you decided to save money and go for a stop-gap repair it is not the firm's fault if further repairs become necessary later on.

One of the factor's duties listed in the Model Conditions is that he should investigate complaints of unsatisfactory work. Owners should report the repairs as soon as possible and the factor can, if necessary, arrange for a professional report to be done on the work. You would have to pay for the report but, if the repair was a large one, it could save you money in the long run.

Often, the first time owners complain about the work is when they get their half-yearly bill and by this time the firm will already have been paid. This makes it more difficult because it is up to you to try to get your money back. Legally the compensation is owed to you as owners, but the factor will be able to take steps on your behalf. If it involves him in extra expense you will be charged for this.

If the factor fails to get any satisfaction for you, you will have to think about taking legal action. Get professional advice before you go ahead with this because, if you lose, you will have to pay the firm's legal costs as well as your own. (See chapter 3 about going to court.)

WHATEVER HAPPENS, WIN OR LOSE, YOU CAN INSTRUCT THE FACTOR NOT TO USE THAT FIRM AGAIN.

REMEMBER, TOO, THAT IF THE FACTOR HAS ALREADY PAID THE BILL YOU STILL HAVE A DUTY TO PAY YOUR SHARE TO THE FACTOR.

Paying the factor is discussed in the next chapter.

7

The factor's bill

Bills are usually sent out twice a year, though a few factors are now sending them out every three months. This is better for the owners, not only because it is easier to budget if the bills are more regular, but also because after a long time it is difficult to remember what repairs were done.

From the factor's point of view more frequent billing means higher administrative costs and so if you insist on quarterly bills you might have to pay a small extra charge in the management fee.

The factor's bill consists of a number of things and will usually contain the following:

* ground burdens

* insurance (this is discussed in chapter 9)

* the factor's fee for managing the property

* repairs

If you have recently bought the flat you might also be asked for a float. This is explained later in the chapter.

Ground burdens and feu duty

This is usually a very small part of the bill. Ground burdens, or feu duty, are payments which were imposed by the original landowner when the land was first sold for building. It is the factor's duty to collect that money from the owners, usually twice a year, and pay it to the person or organisation who now holds the feu.

Many owners have now "redeemed" their feu duties. That means they have bought out their obligation to pay feu duties. If you have redeemed your feu duty or if it has been redeemed by the previous owner it should no longer appear as an item on the factor's bill.

The factor's management fee

The management fee is the factor's charge for managing the tenement. It covers staff time, telephone calls, letters and travel costs, etc.

Many owners would be happier about the management fee if they knew more about what the factor actually does. It is in the interests of both factor and owners if they discuss these things. Problems arise again and again because of lack of communication between factor and owners.

The amount of fee to be charged should be reached by agreement with the factor, though it is more common for the factor to set the fee himself and include it on your bill. If you are not happy with the amount you can ask him to lower it. If he refuses to do so you must either pay up, change your factor or do without a factor at all. Remember that you cannot as an individual refuse to accept the management fee. All the owners, or a majority of them if that is what your title deeds require, must act as a group on this matter.

Several people complained to us that the management fee was raised without warning. The factor cannot insist on higher payments unless it is agreed beforehand with the owners. It is up to you as a group to decide whether or not to accept the increase, but please remember that it is reasonable for the factor's fees to go up regularly to keep pace with inflation.

The other thing to bear in mind is that the factor will charge more for extra services. For example, if you want him to do regular annual maintenance inspections of the building or if you want to be billed every three months rather than twice a year, it would be reasonable for him to charge more.

Factors do not all charge the same amount. Until a few years ago there was a recommended standard fee for factors in Glasgow but both the Price Commission and the Monopolies and Mergers Commission criticised this practice because they thought it reduced competition between factors and prevented owners from looking for the cheapest service.

Each factor now sets his own management fee and so you can shop around to compare charges. As with anything else, however, cheapest is not always best. You should compare not only prices but also what services you are getting for your money.

Repairs

The biggest part of the bill is usually your share of the repairs. It is also the most unpopular part. You will want to be sure that the accounts are accurate. If the bill does not give a breakdown of each job done and you are uncertain that it is right, you can get more information by going along to the factor's office. Every owner has the right to inspect the detailed accounts of each job.

I've been charged for work in a neighbour's house

Factors do sometimes make mistakes and bill you for someone else's share of the work, but make certain of your facts before leaping in with a complaint.

You are only responsible for a share in the costs of maintaining and repairing the common parts of the building, such as the stairs, the external walls, the roof, the main entrance, and so on as laid down in your title deeds. It is not generally your duty to pay for work done inside another owner's house. For example, let us say that dry rot starts near the back entrance, spreads into the close and then into one of the ground floor flats. You are responsible for a share in the costs of removing the rot from the back entrance and close but NOT for work inside the ground floor flat unless you are the owner of that flat. So too, any roof repairs that need done should be shared between you, but if the roof was in such a state that someone's ceiling fell in that unfortunate owner would have to foot her own bill for a new ceiling. In some cases, however, the owner would be able to show that negligence of the other owners caused the damage to her flat and so get compensation that way.

Occasionally, however, work done inside one person's flat is a common repair and the cost should be shared by everyone, for example if the work was to do with common plumbing arrangements.

I've been billed for work that wasn't done

It may seem extraordinary but this does occasionally happen. We have heard of several such complaints from owner-occupiers.

One told us: "My husband who is a joiner himself removed the skirting boards to allow the plumbers easy access. But on the bill there appeared the item 'removal of skirting board'."

Another said: "A few months ago the guttering on the roof was repaired and we paid for it. Recently there has been leaking again at the back. A friend of mine who is a builder went up and had a look at it and said there was no new guttering on the back, although there was on the front. But we were charged for both."

Sometimes these allegations are true but more often than not the owners have simply forgotten that a repair was done because it was so long ago. Sometimes also they did not know about it because they were out at work or at the shops when the tradesmen were working.

There are several ways of preventing these misunderstandings. Quarterly bills would mean that the delay between the work being done and the owners paying for it would not be so long. Getting consulted on big jobs beforehand is also a help. We heard of one stair in Glasgow where the owners managed to get a work-card system going to check on repairs. Each owner keeps a record of any fault he reports, when he complains to the factor about it and when the work is done. Such a system would also protect factors because they would not get criticisms about work not having been done just because the owners have forgotten about it.

There are cases where owners are wrongly billed for work that hasn't been done and this is usually the fault of the tradesman charging for more jobs than he actually did. Sometimes the firm genuinely believed that the work was done. For example, in the case of the woman whose husband removed the skirting board for the plumbers, the firm might not have been told that their own tradesmen did not do that part of the job.

Should I pay for work that hasn't been done?

Strictly speaking if the factor has already paid the firm you have a duty to pay the factor. Tell him about the mistake, however, and ask him to raise it with the firm. If he doesn't get your money back for you it would be necessary for the owners to contact the firm as a group.

Chapter 3 has a section on unsatisfactory work that might be useful to read.

Should I pay for work that is badly done?

Again you have to pay the factor if he has already paid the bill but you should ask him to complain to the firm for you.

If the factor has not yet paid the bill you are in a much stronger negotiating position. Make sure that in future the factor is asked to inspect work before paying the tradesmen. You can also insist that he does not use that same firm again.

How to get your money back if the work is unsatisfactory is described more fully in Chapter 3.

Do we have to pay for work we are not happy with?

Legally the factor is your agent and can take decisions on your behalf. For that reason, if he instructs tradesmen and pays them for the work he is acting on your authority EVEN IF YOU WERE NOT CONSULTED BEFOREHAND.

That is why it is much better to reach an agreement in writing with your factor that he should consult you beforehand on big jobs, should provide several estimates and should inspect the work before paying the bill. Getting him to do these extra tasks might cost a little more in management fees but it could be money well spent.

Even though you may have to pay the factor (unless he manages to get the money back for you from the firm) you still have the right to complain to the firm yourselves and if need be take court action against them.

I've been asked to pay a float. What is it?

Your bill may include a float, which can be anything between £15 and £150. It is an amount to help the factor with his cashflow problems, especially as he may have to wait some time after the bills have been paid before getting the owners' money in. The factor will be out of pocket until you pay him and he knows that getting money from some owners is more difficult than from others.

The float is a one-off payment and you will normally be asked for it when you first buy the house. Occasionally another float is asked for to keep up with inflation but this certainly should not be done every year. When you sell the house you should get your float back.

Owners do not have to agree to paying a float if they do not want to, but such a decision would have to be reached by the owners as group, not just by you yourself. And if you refuse to pay a float the factor may well withdraw his services. Most factors nowadays are unwilling to work without the owners paying a float.

If you have signed the Model Conditions you will already have agreed to pay a float. But remember, you should ask for your float back when you sell the house.

My neighbour won't pay the factor's bill

Really it is a problem between the factor and the individual owner if one refuses to pay the bill. The factor has the right to chase him up for the money and, if need be, take him to court.

In practice, however, some factors simply give up on the property if there are several bad payers. This won't help you at all because there will be delays in getting work done, disagreements between the owners and bad feeling between factor and owners.

For example, one owner told us: "The factor refuses to administer for any repair other than burst pipes as he claims that one of the owners defaulted in payment for a repair in the past."

It must be said that a factor who takes this attitude is not doing his job properly and certainly should not be charging the other owners the full management fee. It is his job to help with the smooth running of the property. Owners in this position are entitled to demand that the factor organises repairs as necessary or else dismiss the factor. Dismissing the factor is explained in chapter 5.

But that doesn't solve the problem of the bad payer. If you have already organised a system of the owners getting together to discuss problems, this is one of the things you can raise. Persuasion from the other owners might help though sometimes it can lead to even more ill-feeling.

Some owners may genuinely be unable to afford repairs. Read chapter 10 for details about grants and loans.

Can I be forced to pay my neighbour's share?

There is some legal doubt about this question. There are two main opinions but, since the issue has never been tested in court, we cannot give an absolute yes or no answer.

The factors argue that, as the owners' agent, the debt is not really owed to the factor but to the other owners. If the factor takes the bad payer to court he is acting on behalf of the other owners. Following from this, some factors refuse to take action against an individual owner and instead share his part of the bill out among the others.

If this happens to you, take legal advice. As owners you would have the right to take the bad payer to court to get your money back, but this takes time and money. You would have to decide whether or not it was worth it. It would certainly not have much chance of success if the factor had already taken the owner to court and lost.

The other legal opinion is that the factor does NOT have the right to spread the debts among the other owners because you are responsible only for your own flat's share, you have paid your obligation to the factor and his agreement with another owner is not your concern. There may be a difference between repair bills and the factor's management fee.

To avoid disputes like this it is sensible to have a written agreement with your factor stating clearly what should happen if one or several owners do not pay their bills. The Factors Association's Model Conditions state that the factor should take legal proceedings to recover the debt. If he succeeds but the debt is not paid within 21 days the factor can ask the other owners to each pay a proportion of the debt. It would then be up to the other owners to try to get their money back from the bad payer.

This is useful because at least it is written down and everyone knows what should happen if one owner does not pay up. There may be things you want to change in it, however. Twenty-one days is not a very long time for someone in financial difficulties to pay up and you might want to extend it if the factor agrees.

8
Making factoring work better for you

Some of the problems we have been talking about in the last three chapters would not arise if there was proper communication amongst the owners themselves and between factor and owners. Owners sometimes don't know what the factor is doing or even what he is supposed to be doing. This leads to complaints, some of which are really rooted in a misunderstanding of the factor's role. Factors, on the other hand, claim that some owners don't care and that some won't even pay the bills.

Neither factors nor owners can have it both ways. If owners want to be involved they can't expect to sit back waiting for the factor to do everything. Factors complain that the owners leave everything to them, but for years many factors have run things with little consultation.

Opening the lines of communication

Once owners start ignoring factors' letters and factors start ignoring owners' complaints, communications have definitely broken down. But the first step if you really want effective communication between factor and owners is to get some sort of communication amongst the owners themselves.

Many owners never see each other at all. They may work different hours, have different hobbies and interests and have a different approach to life. Some may not live in the building but may rent out their flat. The one thing you have in common is that you all own a flat in the same building. It is important to realise that and that you can get things done more effectively if you work together. It is absurd for one owner to write complaining to the factor about a job that was done, while another writes saying that the first job was never done at all and refusing to pay that part of the bill. Not one of them knows what the other is doing.

Getting together can solve a lot of duplication and problems. Obviously you do not want to meet every week to discuss the management of the property — if you took every decision yourselves it would hardly be worth paying for the services of a factor. Some people, however, have found that by meeting each other and taking decisions they have ended up doing the factor's job and have decided to dismiss him and go it alone. The pros and cons of using a factor are weighed up at the end of the end of this chapter.

Let's assume that you do want to continue using a factor. Even with a factor it is important for owners to get together, at least occasionally. You will want to discuss complaints about the factor's services, the standard of work done, the costs involved and any delays that you feel are unnecessary. On a more positive front you will also want to discuss what improvements you would like to see to the property, how much you feel able to spend on them, and what kind of things you would like to see in a written agreement with the factor.

Another important reason for holding meetings is that under the title deeds of your property (explained in chapter 1) it is very difficult for one owner alone to insist on work being done. Most factored flats allow for decisions to be reached if a majority agree to them but occasionally all the owners must agree before anything is done. So, without the agreement of your neighbours you cannot insist on a repair being done or try to change the terms of your agreement with the factor, and so on.

Some flat owners with factors have set up owners' associations which meet regularly and have written constitutions. It is useful to get the factor to attend these meetings and it could be part of his job to organise them. After all, the whole point of having a factor is to save you time and effort.

Newsletters can be another important source of communication between owners. Some factors already send out regular news sheets but so far it tends to happen mainly in modern blocks of flats. Something similar could be done in any flatted property, even on a smaller scale.

Reaching an agreement with your factor

Once the owners have got together and know what they are looking for it is useful to have the factor along at a meeting. He might be surprised that the owners are showing so much interest after such a long period of apathy. If he is a good factor, he should be pleased to attend. Better co-operation is in his interests too.

Many owners will have already signed the Factors' Association's Model Conditions and this is a good basis to work on. Even if you have signed, the agreement can still be renegotiated between factor and owners if there are some terms you would like to see changed.

Some owners may have no written agreement with their factor at all and this is an ideal opportunity to work out with the factor an agreement that is acceptable to both parties. If, however, the factor does not agree to getting written agreement or tries to force you to accept the Model Conditions without any changes at all, you will have to decide whether to accept his terms or dismiss him and get a more sympathetic factor. But it works both ways. You should not expect the factor to accept everything on your terms. He is not looking after your property on the grounds of charity.

What should be in our agreement with the factor?

PAYMENT — This should include the management fee and what work it should cover. If, for example, you want regular inspections or quarterly bills, the fee might be slightly higher but it should all be clearly stated in the agreement.

You will have to agree how often bills are to be sent out, whether or not a float is required and how much that should be per owner. Also you will have to agree on how the advances of money are banked — should you get the interest or should the factor? Then there is the problem of the bad payer. You have to agree with the factor who is responsible for chasing up the money and perhaps taking the owner to court, and whether or not that owner's share will be spread among the other owners.

INSPECTIONS — You should agree with the factor how often inspections to the property should be carried out to see what repairs or improvements might be required. The question of an inspection after jobs have been done is also important. Should every job be inspected or only major ones? You want to make sure that the factor does not pay tradesmen's bills until the work has been looked at.

ORDERING REPAIRS — What degree of consultation do you want before work is ordered? You will probably want to fix a lower cost limit below which the factor can go ahead and order minor jobs without contacting all the owners, but for more expensive repairs you will want to specify the number of estimates you want to see beforehand and clarify whether or not the factor will use estimates obtained from the owners.

In an emergency, instant action is necessary. The agreement should make it clear that the factor can order immediate repairs in this situation.

INVESTIGATING COMPLAINTS — Will it be one of the factor's jobs to investigate complaints of bad workmanship? If the complaints are well-founded will he take legal action on behalf of the owners?

INSURANCE — One of the factor's jobs is usually to take out insurance on behalf of the owners. You might want to state what type of insurance you prefer. Chapter 9 discusses insurance.

MEETINGS AND NEWSLETTERS — Do you want the factor to arrange meetings? If so, how often? And do you want him to send out regular information about the property?

This list is not meant to include everything. For example, in some flats the service includes cleaning, caretaking, security arrangements and lift maintenance as well as repairs. This is more common in modern properties and obviously costs much more.

Remember that anything extra you are asking the factor to do will mean higher management fees but in most cases you will be getting a better service.

The Property Owners and Factors Association of Glasgow, as has been explained earlier, has brought out a document outlining their suggested Model Conditions for factoring. A copy is in the Appendix to this booklet. No groups of owners have to accept the Model Conditions but there are many worthwhile conditions in it and it could act as a useful negotiating point between factors and owners.

The pros and cons of factoring

Factoring

You get someone else to see to all the work that needs to be done. This saves you time and a lot of hassle, especially if some of the other owners are apathetic about the property.

Doing It Yourselves

You have to do everything yourselves, get agreement for repairs, get various estimates and compare them, and make sure that the work is done properly.

The factor can take decisions on your behalf — and make you pay for them. BUT you can try to get agreement from him on what work should be done, and what firms to use.

You have complete control over what jobs need to be done, what firms to use and how much you can afford to spend on the work.

Besides repair bills you have to pay the factor a management fee.

You have no other overheads apart from stationery, stamps and so on.

The factor will have a good knowledge about which firms to use and which to avoid. BUT he may use the same old firms time and time again even if they are no use. The factor is also likely to have contacts in other fields such as surveying if you need a specialist report.

You have complete choice over what firms to use but you won't have specialised knowledge about the best people for the job or know which firms are cowboys. Consultation with other associations who have used tradesmen is essential but it takes time.

If some owners don't pay up the factor will usually try to get the money from them directly without involving you. BUT he could eventually ask you to pay the unpaid share of the bills.

You are faced with a difficult situation if some owners refuse to co-operate or to pay their share. It is up to you as owner occupiers to try to get the money back, if need be by taking court action. In the meantime you have to pay the tradesman's bills yourself or you too could be faced with legal action.

In theory factoring may be the better system, but in practice there are almost as many problems as exist when people are trying to do it themselves. It all boils down to one thing — commitment from all the owners. Without the participation (and willingness to pay) of all the owners neither system can work with complete success.

If, however, people are keen to make a go of it the choices are very real. Doing it yourselves takes a lot of time and effort but at least you are in control of the situation. On the other hand, factoring can be more expensive (though the factor may save you from making some expensive mistakes) but at least it saves the owners spending their own valuable time inspecting the property, getting estimates, ordering work and collecting money.

If the owners ARE all committed you should be demanding a better service from your factor, more communication, more consultation and written terms that are agreeable to both of you. To make this work effectively you would have to pay a higher fee than is presently common. In the long term it would probably be worth it.

9
Insurance

People are usually glad to have insurance when something goes wrong but groan when it comes round to paying the annual premium.

As a homeowner you will probably have two types of insurance — insurance to cover loss, theft or damage to the CONTENTS of your home and insurance to cover the BUILDING. We deal here only with the insurance of the building — though you may have more than one policy covering this.

Who should take out the insurance?

When you get a mortgage the building society or bank usually insists that you get building insurance. This should cover damage to your own flat and also your share of the common parts of the property. Each individual owner has his or her own insurance, but unfortunately problems can arise if not all the owners are properly insured.

Let us imagine that the property is badly damaged by fire and the roof has to be completely replaced, but it turns out that only three of the eight owners have proper insurance. Two have no insurance at all. The other three were insured but had ignored the warnings from their insurance companies to increase their premiums in line with inflation. Their insurance companies will, therefore, pay only part of their share.

The end result could be that repair work is delayed for months while those who were not properly insured look for other ways to pay their share of the cost.

One way of overcoming this problem is to have ONE insurance policy which covers individual flats and the common parts. Each owner pays only a share of the premiums. If the policy is a good one and the amount you have insured the building for is high

enough, this method will ensure that every owner has adequate insurance protection.

Owners with factors will find that there is already a common insurance policy arranged by the factor. His duty to do this is usually laid down in the title deeds. The factor collects each owner's share of the premium and pays it to the insurance company.

Need I pay both my own insurance and the factor's?

Many owners complain when they see insurance on the factor's bill because they are already paying an insurance policy of their own. They feel they are paying twice for the same protection.

In many cases you are and there is very little you can do about it. You are obliged by your building society or bank to take out your own policy, but the title deeds also oblige you and the other owners to have a common policy which is usually arranged by the factor. Sometimes the common policy has been allowed to dwindle to a very low level and the amount the property is insured for is much less than is necessary. This creates no problems if every owner has his own sound individual insurance but it can lead to difficulties if some owners are not adequately insured.

And you still have to pay your share of the common premium even if you feel that you yourself have an excellent insurance policy.

One possible solution would be to end individual policies and get a much better common policy covering all the risks. Most common policies at the moment are inadequate and so you would have to make sure that the policy would cover much more. You would also have to be prepared to pay the higher premiums that would result.

What would happen to your individual policy that the building society made you take out? It seems foolish to pay twice for the same thing. The Scottish Consumer Council contacted many banks and building societies and all said that they would be willing to allow the owner to take out a share of a common policy rather than their own individual policy, PROVIDED THE COMMON POLICY OFFERED ADEQUATE COVER — though they may charge a fee for accepting this change.

Common insurance policies are more usual in modern blocks of flats and, because they tend to give good cover, they are accepted by banks and building societies. There is no reason why this should not be done with older tenements too.

What are the advantages of a common insurance policy?

Provided the policy is adequate, you will all be sure that the building is properly insured and work will not be held back because some owners are inadequately insured. The other main advantage is that only one insurance company has to be dealt with when a claim is made rather than several. This too should speed up the process and cut down on complications and duplication.

What should be in a good policy?

Insurance policies differ a great deal and not all insure you against every risk. The main risks that should be covered are fire, storm, flooding, being hit by vehicles, falling trees, trains or aircraft, subsidence, malicious damage and your liability to compensate someone who has been injured on the property. Not every insurance policy covers all these things. The more risks covered the higher the premium.

The most important part of the policy is the amount the property is insured for. It is tempting to go for a low figure so that your premiums are lower. But it is also dangerous because if anything happens you might not be fully protected and will have to pay part of the costs yourselves.

Many people have their home insured for its market value — how much it would probably fetch if it went up for sale. But this is not good enough because most insurance companies demand that a house should be insured for the amount it would cost to rebuild it if it was completely destroyed. Building societies insist on this replacement value insurance.

Does it matter if I am under-insured?

It certainly does matter, even if the house is not completely destroyed. If you are under-insured the insurance company will probably pay only a part of your claim if the property is damaged or needs to be repaired. Sometimes they may refuse to pay anything at all.

For example, let's say that your house is insured for £10,000 but the insurance company estimates that the rebuilding costs would be £40,000. The roof is damaged in a storm and the repair bill comes to £2,000. The insurance company may pay you only £500 because, they will argue, you have insured it for only a quarter of the amount you should have done.

It is important to increase the amount insured regularly to keep in line with inflation and rising property and building costs. Most insurance companies send out reminders like this and some now offer policies which are index-linked and go up each year automatically with inflation. This means of course that the premium goes up too.

Get advice from an insurance broker on the best insurance policy for your needs. This is especially important if the owners have got together and decided to arrange a common insurance policy or to get the common policy arranged by their factor improved. If you do have a factor, invite him to the meeting. He will be able to advise on policies and will probably be able to arrange it for you.

10
Financial help

Repairs and maintenance cost money. If some owners seem unco-operative it may be that they simply cannot afford expensive repairs and improvements. But there are sometimes ways of getting money to help with the costs. The following are the main ways of getting financial help.

* Repairs grants from the district council

* Improvement grants from the district council

* Loans from the district council

* Increasing your mortgage

* Loans from the bank

* Loans from finance companies

* Help for those on supplementary benefit.

Repairs Grants

The district council can give grants to help with the cost of essential repairs. Grants are by no means given automatically and there are certain things the council will want to be sure of before approving the grant.

* When the repair is done the building should satisfy certain building requirements. For example, you will not get a grant just for roof repairs if the down pipes need to be replaced and are causing dampness. In these cases the council usually insists that you do all the work necessary and will give you a grant towards the total costs.

*   The rateable value of the flat must not be too high. The upper limit varies from district to district and ranges from about £330 to £420. This upper limit does NOT apply if you want to remove lead piping leading to your drinking tap.

*   You will not get a grant if the council thinks you could pay for it yourself without undue hardship. What this means is not spelt out in detail and is operated differently by different councils. You do not have to prove abject poverty but certainly the less well off will be given priority over those with high wages or substantial savings.

Provided these conditions are met the council MUST make a grant if they have served you with a repairs notice. In other cases the council has more discretion whether or not to approve the grant and obviously this will be done on a system of priorities. They may also impose other conditions.

The grant is usually 50 per cent of the cost. You can find out from the district council whether your flat is in a Housing Action Area. Applications can be made by individual owner occupiers but when the repair is to the common parts of the building the council prefers to take them all at once. This is something the factor could help to organise on your behalf.

Remember that decisions on grants are not immediate. Councils have at times been inundated with applications and it can take some months (or even longer) for the applications to be processed and approved.

YOU SHOULD NOT START ANY WORK UNTIL THE GRANT IS APPROVED OR YOU WILL NOT GET YOUR MONEY.

Clearly, this poses problems for owners who need a repair done immediately. You have to decide whether you want the repair done right away and are prepared to pay for it all yourselves or whether the repair can wait until the council is able to decide on the grant.

Improvement Grants

Improvement grants are aimed at people without essential amenities like an inside toilet, bath or shower, or hot and cold running water. They can also be given to bring a house up to an acceptable standard or convert a house to provide more accommodation. The house when repaired should be able to provide satisfactory housing for at least another thirty years.

If the grant is for an essential amenity like a bath the council MUST give you the grant provided that the house is otherwise up to the official tolerable standard. There are limits to the amount of grant you can get. For example in 1984 these were £340 for a fixed bath or shower, £430 for a hot and cold water supply at a bath or shower, £130 for a wash-hand basin, £230 for hot and cold water in the basin, £340 for a sink, £290 for hot and cold water at the sink, and £515 for a toilet. You may also be entitled to up to £3,000 for additional work associated with the improvements, though this is reduced to a maximum of £300 if the house isn't likely to last more than 10 years.

People in Housing Action Areas can get 75 per cent of their costs up to a maximum of £11,400 for a pre-1914 tenement flat.

These figures change regularly, so check with your district council what the current rates are.

You will not get an improvement grant simply because you want the flat to look nicer. For example, if you want to replace your old sink unit with modern fitted units you will not get a grant if the old sink is perfectly adequate.

Loans

There are various sources from which you can borrow money for repairs to your flat. Some of these are set out below. Before deciding which is best for you you should shop around and find out how much they all cost and what the repayment terms are.

Loans from the council

The district council can give you a loan for repairs and improvements. They don't have to do so and will only give you the loan if they are sure that you are able to repay it. They take a security out on your flat, entitling them to a share of its value if you default on the repayments, so they won't give you a loan if your house is already mortgaged to the hilt.

In some circumstances the council is obliged to give you a loan. For example if they have served a repairs notice or you live in a Housing Action Area and you meet certain other conditions.

Before lending you money the council will want a structural survey of the property. You will have to pay for this. If the property is in poor condition you might not get the loan.

Normally you repay the debt by monthly instalments but sometimes the council is willing to let you repay the interest only, getting their capital back when you sell the house. This is a help to people on supplementary benefit who are not allowed to claim repayments of capital in their weekly benefit but who can get interest payments from social security.

Increasing your mortgage

Try approaching the building society or bank which gave you the mortgage to buy the flat. They are usually fairly sympathetic to owner-occupiers who want to improve the value of their property, though much depends on how tight mortgage funds are at the time you approach them. They are unlikely to increase your mortgage if you are already on the maximum mortgage for your income.

At the moment increasing your mortgage is one of the cheapest ways of getting a loan. You can choose either to increase your monthly repayments or, in some cases, to extend the number of years you have to repay it at no extra monthly cost.

Bank loans

Most banks offer loan facilities to people who bank with them, and also to those who do not have accounts, provided that their income is sufficient to meet the repayments. They are unlikely to give a loan to someone who is unemployed.

Bank loans are more expensive than increasing your mortgage and they also have to be paid back in a shorter time, but if you cannot get an increase in your mortgage they are a useful alternative. The interest you pay on a loan for improvements to your flat qualifies for tax relief.

Finance companies

You may be attracted by advertisements from finance companies offering loans.

Be careful with these offers. The interest rates are higher than a bank or building society and so it is an expensive way of borrowing money. As a last resort, however, you may decide that such a loan is necessary. Make sure that you can afford the repayments.

Some owners are asked to give the loan company a second mortgage over the house. This means that if you fall into arrears your flat could be sold off by the loan company. If you are on a

low income we would suggest that you try to get a loan from the district council before even considering taking such a gamble with your home.

Those on supplementary benefit

People on supplementary benefit do not get an allowance for their mortgage or loan repayments but they are entitled to some extra help.

*   The interest payments you make on your mortgage or any other loans you have taken out to repair or improve the property.

*   The factor's management fee.

*   Feu duty if you are still paying it.

*   An extra £1.70 a week to cover insurance and essential minor routine maintenance. Please check with your local social security office in case this rate has gone up by the time you read this.

The small weekly additions are not meant to cover large repairs and you are entitled to apply for help with these. The maximum payment of this kind is currently (mid 1984) £325. You don't get the money for improvements, only for repairs, and the work must be essential to keep the flat habitable.

THIS EXTRA HELP APPLIES ONLY TO PEOPLE ON SUPPLEMENTARY BENEFIT. If you are on unemployment benefit, a widow's pension or sickness benefit and so on you will not get these extra payments unless you are also getting supplementary benefit.

Whether or not you already receive supplementary benefit, if you are having problems meeting the cost of maintaining your property you may be eligible for some help.

Advice about welfare benefits is available at social security offices, social work offices and advice centres.

11
Getting advice

Getting information and advice is absolutely crucial if you want to manage and maintain your property better. We hope that this guide will help you to some extent but it is really only a pointer in the right direction and in some cases much more detailed help is needed with a specific problem.

Other owners' associations

Talking to other owners who have faced similar problems is often the best source of information and help. You can learn from their experiences, their mistakes and their successes.

Some areas also have residents' groups or amenity associations which you might like to join. If there is no such group in your area, why don't you and your neighbours start one?

If you live in Glasgow you could also contact the Federated Association of Owner Occupiers. In Edinburgh the New Town Conservation Committee has done a lot of work on maintenance of tenement buildings, not only in the New Town area. Information about these and other existing groups can be found in your local library or from a Citizens' Advice Bureau.

Community councils

Community councils are statutory bodies whose members are elected from the local people. The areas they cover are fairly small and some of them have gathered information about local housing problems. They might be able to take up a problem you raise with them, for example, if your district council has been slow to force owners to do essential repairs, the community council might be able to take it up with them.

Names and addresses of people on your community council are available from the district or island council. If you live in Glasgow contact the Community Council Resource Centre,

13 John Street, Glasgow. Their telephone number is 041-227 4572 or 041-227 4723.

Advice centres

There are Citizens' Advice Bureaux throughout Scotland and they offer a wide range of information on a number of subjects. If you need further legal advice an appointment can be made for you to see a solicitor and the Bureau will be able to advise on whether or not you are entitled to help with your legal costs.

You will find the address and telephone number of your nearest Bureau in the telephone directory. Or contact the Scottish Association of Citizens' Advice Bureaux in Glasgow, Edinburgh, or Inverness.

Many other organisations provide advice and information centres for the public. Some are run by local authorities, some by voluntary bodies like Shelter, and many by local community groups. They are far too numerous to list here, but a library or community worker should be able to put you in touch with your nearest one.

Solicitors

In some cases you will find that only expert legal advice will help you. Many people are frightened to go to a solicitor in case it costs too much, but there are schemes to help people on low incomes. In any case, when you bought your flat you probably had to use a solicitor and he or she might be happy to give you some extra advice at the time or later for little extra charge. Most solicitors operate a scheme providing 30 minutes of advice for £5 (called the Fixed Fee Interview Scheme).

If you see this sign you know that the solicitor offers a free or cheap service to those on low incomes:

There are two main schemes.

* Legal advice and assistance

* Legal aid.

Legal advice and assistance

Most solicitors operate a scheme whereby you can get advice, information, letters written on your behalf and so on, either free of charge or at a reduced fee, if you have a low income and little savings. People on supplementary benefit or family income supplement get this service free of charge. Others on low incomes pay either nothing at all or else make a contribution to the fees according to their incomes and their responsibilities. There are leaflets in most advice centres which explain how you work out how much you would have to pay.

This scheme does not cover the costs of the lawyer going to court for you.

Legal aid

Legal aid is designed for people who are either taking court action or defending court action. To qualify you must show that your income and savings are low enough and ALSO that you have a reasonable chance of winning. You won't get legal aid for hopeless court actions.

The legal aid leaflets explain what income levels apply and what outgoings are taken into account. Also ask the solicitor at the start whether or not you are likely to be eligible for legal aid and how much you are likely to get.

Only individuals can get legal aid, not groups of people. So, if the owners need legal advice or need a lawyer to take up their case, it would be sensible to find out if one owner is eligible for help with legal costs and do it initially through him.

THE PROPERTY OWNERS AND FACTORS ASSOCIATION, GLASGOW, LIMITED

MODEL CONDITIONS OF MANAGEMENT
OF PREMISES IN FLATTED PROPERTY

1. In these conditions:—

    "Owner" means the proprietor of any part of flatted property which is or could without substantial alteration be occupied as a separate subject and includes the owner/occupier of any such part and the proprietor of any such part which is let or is unoccupied.

2. Subject to the rights of Owners in relation to their own premises the whole property will be managed by a Factor appointed by the Owners of the premises in the property.

3. The Factor has authority on behalf of all the Owners to instruct and have carried out repairs and maintenance to the common parts of the property provided that the anticipated cost of any one item at the time when it is instructed will not exceed £   or such other sum as shall be agreed between the Factor and the Owners from time to time. Subject as aftermentioned if the anticipated cost of any such item exceeds the above sum it shall be instructed and carried out only when the work has been approved by a majority of the Owners after submission of an estimate or estimates by the Factor and the Factor has been put in funds by the Owners to the full amount of the estimated cost. It shall be within the Factor's discretion to instruct works at a cost exceeding £   if he considers the expense to be justifiable on grounds of health or safety and to recover forthwith the costs thereof on the same basis as under condition 5 hereof.

4. Each Owner of premises in the property will deposit with the Factor the sum of £   or such other sum as shall be agreed between the Factor and the Owners from time to time. This sum will be deposited immediately upon acquisition of his premises as a contribution to finance the cost of common charges. The deposit will be returned when he or his representatives cease to own the premises. No interest shall be paid on the deposit.

5. Each of the Owners will pay to the Factor timeously on demand his appropriate share determined in accordance with the provision of the relevant title deeds of the costs of ground burdens, repairs and maintenance, insurance premiums, common and other charges and factorial and other fees. In the event of the share payable by any Owner remaining unpaid after a demand for payment thereof has been issued by the Factor, the Factor shall be entitled to sue for and recover the same in his own name on behalf of the remaining Owners. If payment is not received by the Factor of the amount of any such share and the expenses as awarded by the Court of obtaining a decree for payment therefor within 21 days after the date of the decree for payment or, in the event of an instalment decree for payment, after the date when the last instalment became due, the amount of such share and expenses shall be paid by the remaining Owners jointly to the Factor, each Owner contributing in proportion to his appropriate share of the original costs, and the remaining Owners will be entitled to recover such amount from the defaulting Owner.

6. When an Owner sells or disposes of his premises he shall forthwith notify the Factor of the date of sale or disposal and the identity of his successor in the ownership of the premises and shall use his best endeavours to persuade his successor to adopt and implement these conditions.

7. The appointment of the Factor may be terminated by the Owners or the Factor upon giving not less than three months' prior notice in writing.

8. Decisions by the Owners as to appointment of the Factor or termination of his office or as to the authorisation or approval of repairs or maintenance or as to the type and amount of insurance cover shall be made in accordance with any procedure specified in the relevant title deeds, or, if such procedure is not specified in the title deeds or is not in fact operated, by a majority in number of the Owners of premises in the property whose decision shall be binding upon all the Owners.

9. Unless otherwise specified in the relevant title deeds for the purpose of approving any item of repairs or maintenance in terms of condition 3 hereof or for making any decision in terms of condition 8 hereof an Owner shall have one vote for each part of the property owned by him and which is occupied by him or is separately occupied by his tenant or is unoccupied.

10. The Factor shall be responsible for effecting and keeping in force the amount of insurance cover which has been determined in accordance with condition 8 hereof and the Owners shall if required by the Factor, make arrangements for immediate provision of the amount of the premiums. The Factor shall have no further or other responsibility in relation to the insurance of the property or any parts thereof.

11. These conditions shall apply and continue to apply to all Owners who accept them notwithstanding that they do not apply or cease to apply to other Owners of premises in the same property.

12. The Factor shall undertake the Factorial Duties set out in the Schedule annexed, but nothing in the said Schedule shall impose or imply any liability upon the Factor to Owners or other persons for his failure to instruct repairs on his own initiative following a visit to the property.

SCHEDULE of Factorial Duties referred to in the foregoing

Model Conditions of Management of Premises in Flatted Property

(a) He will make†   visits to the property and take appropriate action to deal with any
(† Insert number or descriptive word e.g. periodic as agreed with owners)
matters of a common or mutual nature which are discovered.

(b) Unless contractors are nominated by Owners he will order repairs to firms which, from his ex-perience, he believes to be reliable and capable of completing the repairs satisfactorily and at a reasonable cost. When appropriate he will when instructing repairs consult with the Contractors as to the type of repair and the materials to be used.

(c) Where a repair requires the services of more than one Trade he will arrange for the several firms of tradesmen to co-ordinate their work.

(d) Where he considers it to be in the interests of the Owners he will obtain estimates from several tradesmen for the same job, advise the Owners and obtain their instructions before proceeding.

Where the proposed repair is mutual to an adjoining building he will negotiate with the adjoining Owners or Factor and endeavour to ensure that the work is completed satisfactorily at a reasonable cost and that the adjoining owners pay their share of the cost. He will not instruct such work without such agreement unless he is so authorised by his own Owners.

(e) He will investigate any complaints of unsatisfactory work. Owners will assist here by reporting any such complaints to the Factor as soon as possible. Where considered necessary and if so instructed by the Owners the Factor will arrange for a professional report on the completed repair. Fees will be chargeable to the Owners.

(f) He will check the Tradesmen's Accounts when rendered, including the charge of V.A.T., will calculate the share of the cost due by each owner in the building and unless otherwise agreed will issue half yearly accounts to each Owner.

He will also ensure that accounts for ground burdens, insurances and all other outgoings are checked and paid when due. He will calculate the shares due by each Owner and include same in the half yearly accounts.

(g) On appointment the Factor will agree the management charge with the Owners and such charge will be revised as necessary from time to time thereafter. Such revisions will not normally be made more frequently than once a year. The management fee as agreed from time to time will cover routine management duties but it is understood that if because of the complexity of a particular repair or because of any other reason the Factor is involved in extra work an additional fee may be chargeable.

(h) When a change of ownership takes place the Factor will on request make the necessary apportion-ment of ground burdens, insurances, repairs and other outgoings between the seller and the purchaser. Any charge for this additional work will be payable by the Seller.

(i) If requested he will arrange to supply one photostat copy of Tradesmen's accounts to one owner per building each half year.

(j) He will guide and assist Owners in submitting applications for grants towards the cost of common repairs or improvements.

(k) In the event of any court action being raised on behalf of the Owners by or against any third party instructions will first be taken from the Owners as they will be liable for all legal costs not re-covered.

Note: Those duties marked with an asterisk (*) are considered to be outwith routine management and an additional fee as appropriate will be chargeable by the Factor.

(Name and Address of Factor)   (For office use)

I agree that the Model Conditions and Schedule shall apply in respect of my premises in the property

signed ....

address ....

....

date ....

INDEX

Walls

© Crown copyright 1984
First published 1984

Illustrations by 'Larry'.

Printed in the UK for HMSO. Dd. 762018/4475 C150 11/84 (13218).